Scrap Paper Journeys

Desert Cactus Designs

Boho Hippie Dog Collection

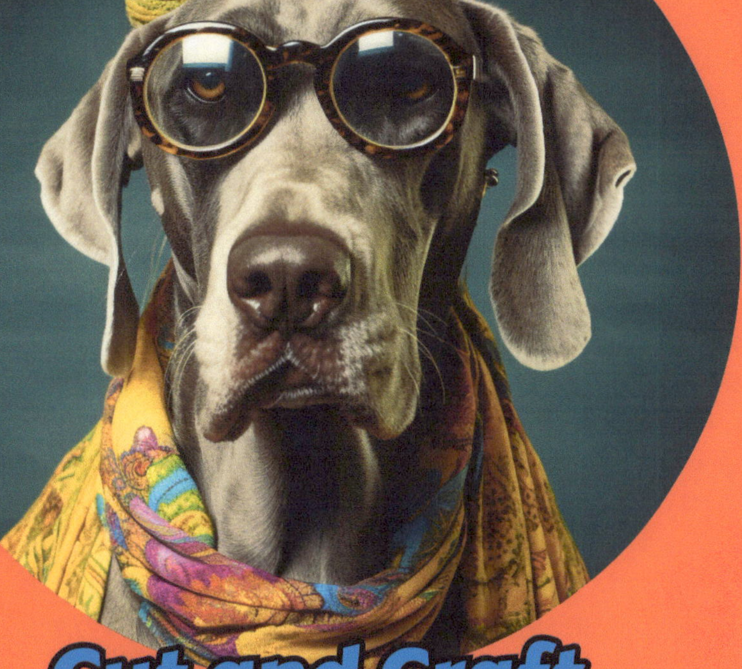

Cut and Craft

This picture book of Boho Hippie Dogs is filled with "totally grooy" dogs. This book is made for crafting such as: mixed media art, papercraft art, junk journals, scrapbooking, collage and decoupage as well as card making, gift tags and decorative embellishments.

The pictures are meant inspire your creativity. Pick from the several sizes and shapes to fit your project, cut them out and add the chosen picture to create a truly unique and interesting item.

Have lots of fun on your projects!
Judy

Instructions on how to create a collage:

1. **Gather materials**: Collect materials for your collage such as magazines, newspapers, colored papers, photographs, scissors, glue, and a surface to work on (like a paper or canvas).

2. **Choose a theme or idea**: Decide what you want your collage to represent. It could be a specific topic, a mood, or just a collection of your favorite images.

3. **Prepare your surface**: If you're working on a canvas, ensure it's clean and ready to use. If using paper, choose a size and cut it to fit your preference.

4. **Select images**: Start flipping through your materials and cut out images or patterns that relate to your chosen theme. Feel free to cut out shapes, words, or any other visual elements you find interesting.

5. **Arrange the cutouts**: Begin arranging the cutouts on your surface, experimenting with the composition and placement. Move them around until you're satisfied with the overall look.

6. **Glue the cutouts**: Once you're happy with the arrangement, start gluing the cutouts onto the surface one by one. Apply a thin layer of glue to the back of each piece and press it firmly onto the surface.

7. **Layer and overlap**: To add depth and visual interest to your collage, experiment with layering and overlapping the cutouts. This can create unique textures and patterns.

8. **Fill gaps**: Look for any empty spaces between cutouts and fill them by cutting smaller pieces or shapes from your materials. This helps create a cohesive composition.

9. **Add personal touches**: Consider incorporating personal elements such as photographs, handwritten quotes, or drawings. This adds a personal touch and makes the collage more meaningful to you.

10. **Experiment with textures**: Explore different textures by incorporating materials like fabric, ribbon, lace, or textured papers into your collage. This can add tactile interest and make it visually dynamic.

11. **Review and adjust**: Step back and review your collage from a distance. Make any necessary adjustments to ensure the composition is balanced and visually pleasing. You can also trim or modify any elements that aren't working well.

12. **Optional**: Seal or protect your collage: If you wish to preserve your collage or protect it from damage, you can apply a thin layer of clear acrylic sealer or Mod Podge over the surface. Allow it to dry completely before handling or displaying.

13. **Enjoy and display**: Once your collage is complete and any protective layers have dried, take a moment to appreciate your creation. Hang it on a wall, frame it, or display it in any way that brings you joy and allows others to admire your work.

14. **Experiment with variations**: Collage is a versatile art form, so feel free to explore different techniques and styles. Try using different materials, textures, color schemes, or compositions to create unique and diverse collages.

15. **Share your work**: Share your collage with friends, family, or on social media. Receive feedback, inspire others, and celebrate your artistic achievement.

Remember, creating a collage is meant to be a fun and creative process, so don't be afraid to experiment and let your imagination guide you. Enjoy the journey and let your personal expression shine through your collage!

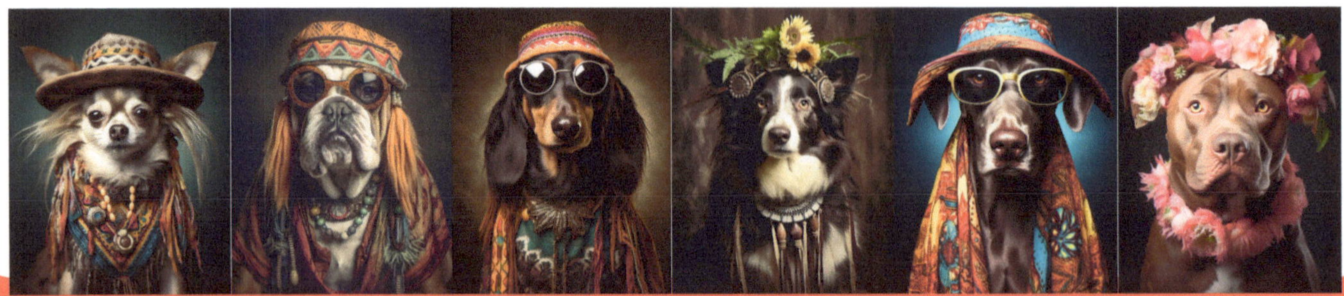

<u>Instructions on how to create a Scrapbook page:</u>

1.**Gather materials**: Collect a variety of materials for your scrapbook page such as photographs, patterned papers, cardstock, embellishments, scissors, adhesive (glue or double-sided tape), markers or pens, and any additional decorative elements you wish to include.

2. **Select a theme or event**: Choose a specific theme or event for your scrapbook page. It could be a vacation, birthday, wedding, or any special moment worth documenting.

3. **Choose background paper**: Pick a color or pattern cardstock that complements your theme and sets the overall tone for your scrapbook page.

4. **Organize and trim photos**: Arrange your selected photos in a pleasing layout on your background paper. Once you're satisfied, trim and crop the photos if needed to fit within the desired space on the page.

5. **Add borders or frames**: Add borders or frames. Cut a piece of coordinating patterned paper or cardstock slightly larger than the photos to adhere the photo on for a frame effect.

6. **Layer patterned papers**: Cut additional pieces of patterned papers or cardstock in different shapes and sizes. Layer these papers behind or beside your photos to create depth and visual interest or to create pockets for hidden journaling or additional photos.

7. **Embellish with stickers or die-cuts**: Add dimension and decoration to your scrapbook page by incorporating stickers, die-cuts, or other embellishments related to your theme.

8. **Include journaling**: Write a brief description or caption to accompany your photos. Use a pen or marker to journal directly on the page or create a separate journaling card to include.

9. **Use decorative elements**: You can use ribbon, washi tape, or other decorative elements to enhance your scrapbook page.

10. **Arrange and adhere everything**: Finalize the layout by arranging all elements on your page. Once you're happy with the arrangement, start gluing or adhering everything down using adhesive.

11. **Review and adjust**: Step back and review your scrapbook page from a distance. Make any necessary adjustments to ensure the composition is balanced and visually appealing.

12. **Add titles and captions**: Consider adding a title or small phrases to your scrapbook page that reflects the theme or event. Use stickers, lettering stickers, or your own handwriting to create the title.

13. **Enhance with additional embellishments**: If desired, enhance your scrapbook page further by adding additional embellishments such as stickers, paper punches, brads, or sequins.

14. **Consider protective covers**: A cover helps to preserve your work and prevent any damage once your scrapbook page is complete by adding a clear plastic sheet or page protector.

15. **Repeat the process**: If you're creating multiple scrapbook pages for a larger album, repeat these instructions for each page following your desired theme or event.

16. **Share and enjoy**: Share your completed scrapbook page with family and friends. Display it in an album, frame it, or share it digitally. Celebrate the memories and the effort you put into creating the page.

17. **Experiment and have fun**: Remember that scrapbooking is a creative and personal process. Don't be afraid to experiment with different layouts, techniques, and materials that inspire you. Enjoy the process and let your creativity flow.

Remember, scrapbooking allows you to tell a story and preserve cherished memories. Have fun and let your creativity shine as you create beautiful and meaningful scrapbook pages to treasure for years to come.

Instructions on how to make a Card:

1. **Gather your materials**: Collect your scrap paper pad, blank cards or cardstock, adhesive (glue or double-sided tape), scissors, and any additional embellishments such as stickers, ribbon, or stamps.

2. **Decide on the size of your card**: Measure and mark the desired size on the scrap paper using a ruler and pencil. A typical card size is around 4x6 inches. Carefully cut out the marked shape using scissors. Once you have your card base, fold it in half vertically. Use the ruler to make sure the crease is straight and sharp. This will create a foldable card.

3. **Now you can get creative and decorate your card**: Select a picture that you'd like to use as the main design element for your card. You can use scrap paper to create patterns or cut out shapes to add to the front of the card. Glue these decorations onto the card base. You can also use markers or pens to add personal messages or drawings.

4. **Inside message**: Open the card and write a personal message on the inside. This can be a handwritten note, a quote, or a heartfelt message for the recipient. This can be done using markers, pens, or even by gluing another piece of scrap paper on the inside to write on.

5. **Outside front of card**: Embellish your card! Get creative with additional embellishments. Consider adding stickers, ribbon, or stamped images that complement the design of the scrap paper. Arrange them on the card front and secure them with adhesive.

6. **Finishing touches:** Review the card and add any final touches. You can further enhance the card by adding stickers, ribbon, or other embellishments. Get creative and personalize it to your liking! Consider using ink to distress the edges of the card or adding a sparkle with glitter glue.

7. **Finish up**: Once you have finished decorating the card, let it dry if you have used glue or any wet materials.

8. **Optional:** Decorate the envelope: If desired, decorate the envelope to match the card. Use coordinating pictures, scrap paper, stamps, or stickers to add flair and make the card presentation even more special.

9. **Review and finalize**: Take a step back and review the card. Make any necessary adjustments to ensure that everything is secure and visually appealing. Be sure to express your sentiments and personalize it for the recipient.

Your scrap paper card is now ready to be shared and cherished! Remember, the beauty of handmade cards lies in their uniqueness, so don't hesitate to experiment, and let your creativity shine.

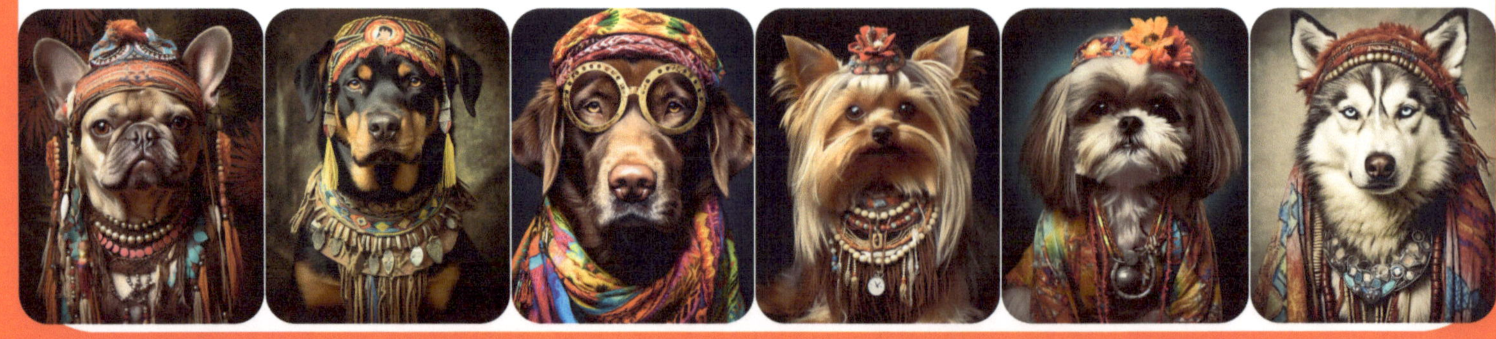

Instructions on how to Decoupage:

1. **Gather materials**: Collect the necessary materials for decoupage, including a base object (such as a wooden box, picture frame, or tray), decorative paper, napkins or photos, decoupage medium (glue/sealer), paintbrushes, scissors, and any additional embellishments you'd like to use.

2. **Prepare the surface**: Ensure that the surface of your base object is clean and dry. If needed, lightly sand and wipe off any dust or debris to create a smooth surface for decoupage.

3. **Cut or tear the paper**: Cut or tear your decorative paper or napkins into small or medium-sized pieces. Experiment with different shapes and sizes to create variety in your design.

4. **Apply decoupage glue**: Use a paintbrush to apply a thin, even layer of decoupage glue/sealer onto a small section of the base object. This will serve as the adhesive for your paper pieces.

5. **Place the paper**: Carefully place one of your cut or torn paper pieces onto the wet glue, smoothing it down with your fingers or a soft brush. Remove any air bubbles or wrinkles as you go.

6. **Continue layering**: Apply another thin layer of decoupage glue/sealer over the first paper piece to act as a sealant. Then, continue applying more glue to the base object in small sections and layering the paper pieces, slightly overlapping them as you go. Repeat this process until you have covered the desired area or achieved the desired design.

7. **Smooth and remove bubbles**: After applying each paper piece, gently smooth it out to ensure it adheres well and eliminate any air bubbles or wrinkles. Use a soft brush or your fingertips to press out any imperfections.

8. **Allow drying time:** Set aside your decoupage project to dry completely. Follow the instructions on the decoupage glue/sealer bottle for the recommended drying time. This step is crucial to ensure the paper adheres properly and the finish is smooth.

9. **Apply additional coats**: Once the initial layer has dried, apply additional coats of decoupage glue/sealer over the entire design. This helps seal the paper, adds durability, and creates a cohesive finish. Allow each coat to dry thoroughly before adding the next.

10. **Seal and protect**: To ensure the longevity of your decoupage project, apply a final layer of decoupage glue/sealer or a clear varnish over the entire surface. This helps protect the paper, seals the design, and adds a glossy or matte finish depending on your preference. Allow it to dry completely.

11. **Cleanup and drying**: Clean any excess sealer from your brushes and work area using warm water and soap. Allow your project to dry in a clean and well-ventilated area away from dust or direct sunlight.

12. **Enjoy and display**: Once your project is completely dry, you can proudly display or use it as desired. You can display it as a decorative piece, gift it to someone special, or incorporate it into your home decor.

13. **Clean and care**: To clean your decoupaged object, simply wipe it gently with a soft cloth or sponge. Avoid immersing it in water or using harsh chemicals, as they can damage the decoupage design. Proper care will help maintain the longevity of your decoupage project.

14. **Experiment and explore**: Decoupage is a versatile art form, so feel free to experiment with different papers, objects, and techniques.

Remember, decoupage allows you to personalize and transform ordinary objects into unique pieces of art. Enjoy the process and let your creativity flow. Each project is an opportunity to express yourself and create something truly special. Embrace the joy of decoupage and share your creations with others to inspire and encourage their creativity. Happy decoupaging!

Instructions on how to create a Junk Journal:

1. **Gather materials**: Collect a variety of pictures and papers such as old book pages, scrapbooking paper, envelopes, junk mail, magazine cutouts. Also, gather additional materials like scissors, glue sticks, markers, ribbon, lace, stickers, and any other embellishments you might want to include.

2. **Choose a size and format**: Decide on the size of your junk journal, such as a standard letter-sized paper or a smaller notebook size. You can also use existing notebooks or journals as a starting point or create your journal from scratch.

3. **Prepare the pages**: Cut or tear the pictures and scrap paper into your desired size or shape for the journal pages. You can create different sizes to add interest and variety.

4. **Arrange and layer**: Start arranging the pages by layering them in any order you like. Mix different types of papers, colors, and textures to create an eclectic look.

5. **Add pockets and envelopes**: To make your junk journal more functional, consider adding pockets or envelopes to store small mementos or keepsakes. Glue down the sides and bottom of an envelope or fold a piece of scrap paper in half and glue down three edges to create a pocket. Attach these to various pages within your journal.

6. **Experiment with different layouts**: Use scrap paper to experiment with the placement of your pages and ephemera. Mix full-page spreads with collages, pockets, and overlays. Don't be afraid to overlap elements or add interactive elements like fold-outs or flip pages with additional scrap paper. This will make your journal visually engaging and interactive.

7. **Add tabs or dividers**: Use tabs or dividers to easily navigate through your journal by using scrap paper. Cut strips of paper and attach them to the edge of specific pages for quick reference to important sections or themes.

8. **Embellish and decorate**: Now comes the fun part! Use your creativity to decorate the pages with images from your scrap paper book, stickers, stamps, washi tape, ribbons, lace, or any other embellishments you desire. You can also write or doodle directly on the pages.

9. **Include journaling prompts and fill your journal**: To make your junk journal more meaningful, consider adding journaling prompts throughout. These can be questions, quotes, or prompts that help inspire reflection and writing.

10. **Start journaling!** Use your junk journal to document memories, write down thoughts and dreams, sketch, add photos, or create collages. Write whatever comes to mind and let your creativity flow. Share your junk journal with others. Show it to friends, family, or even members of a journaling community. Sharing your creativity can inspire others and create a sense of connection and community.

Have fun and enjoy the process. Remember that creating a junk journal is a creative and personal endeavor. Embrace the process and enjoy the journey of expressing yourself through your journal. Don't be afraid to make mistakes, experiment, and let your imagination run wild.

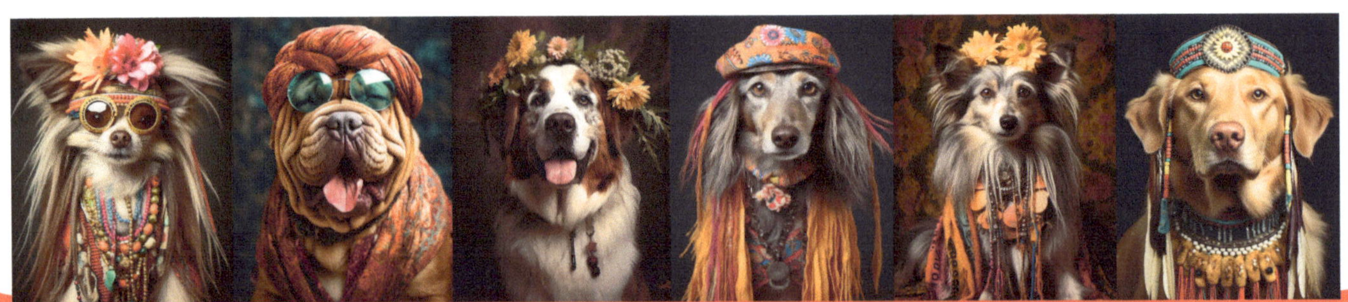

Inspirational Ideas!

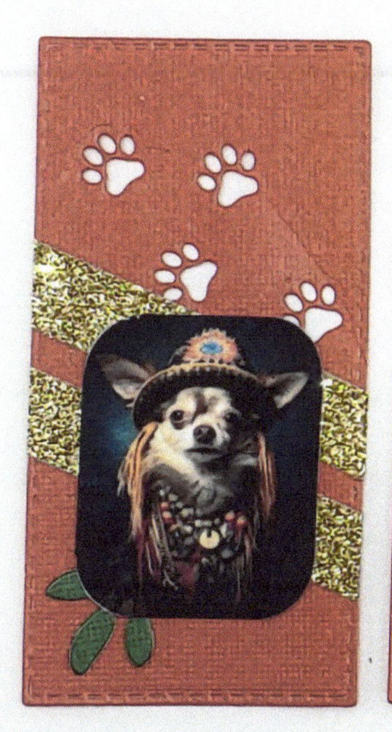 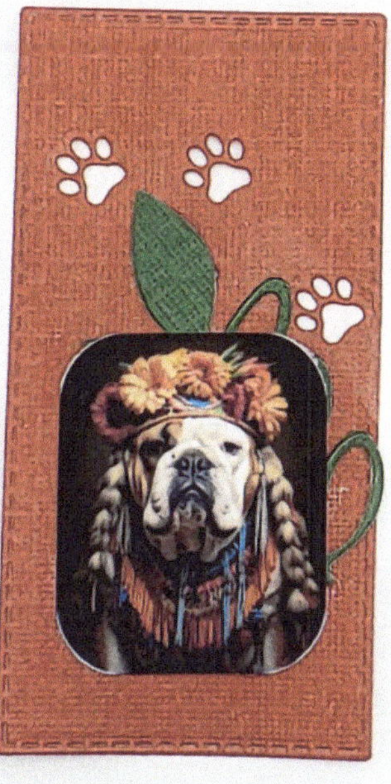 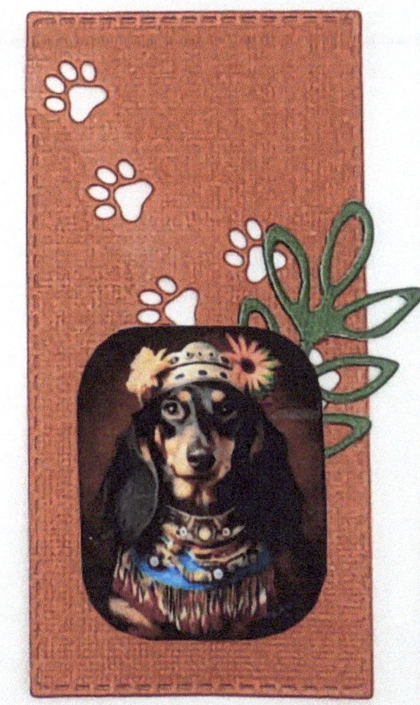 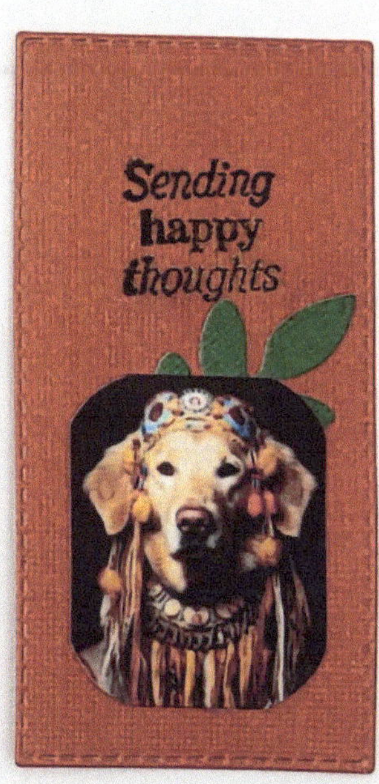

Junk Journal Ephemera and/or Mini Bookmarkers

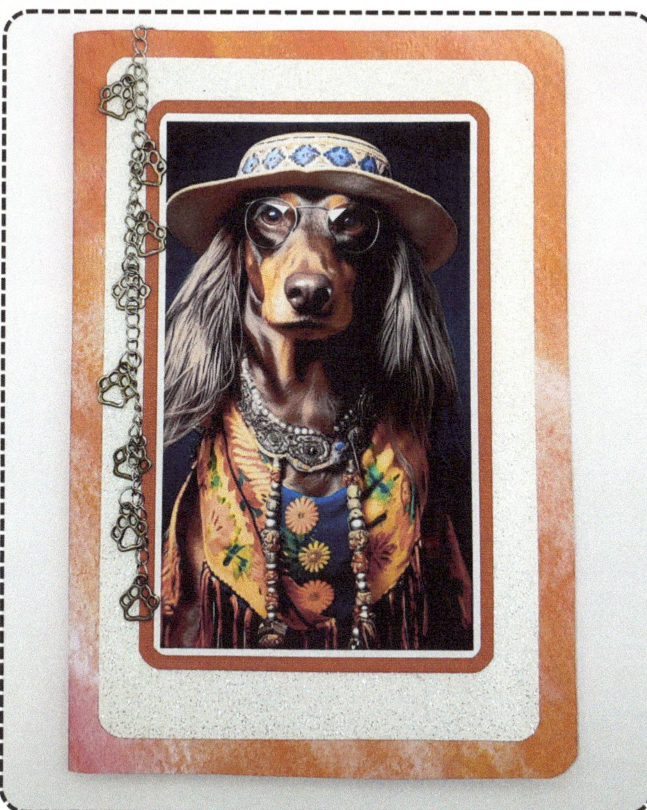

Notebooks

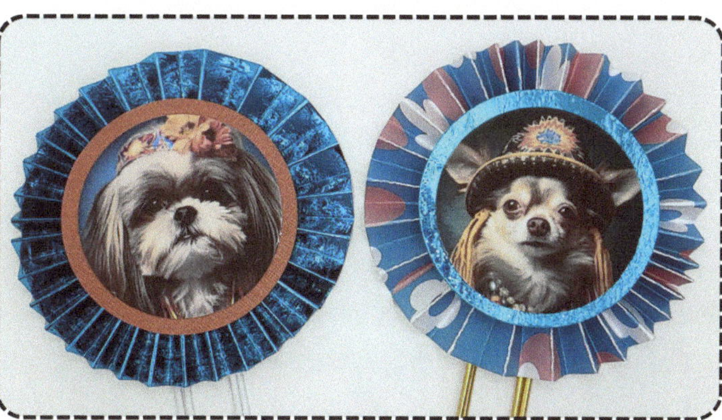

Rosettes for Party Decorations

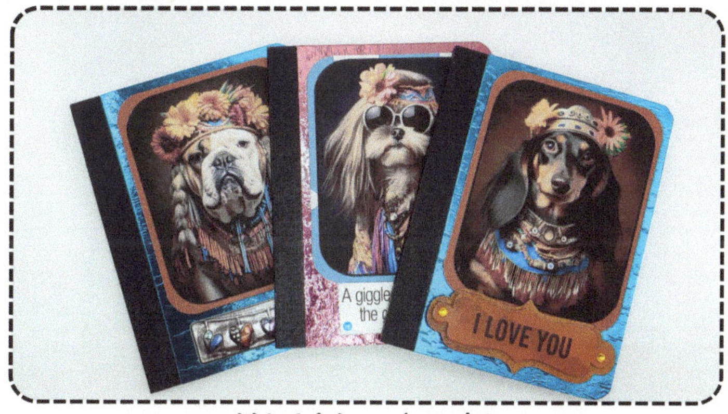

Mini Notebooks

Inspirational Ideas!

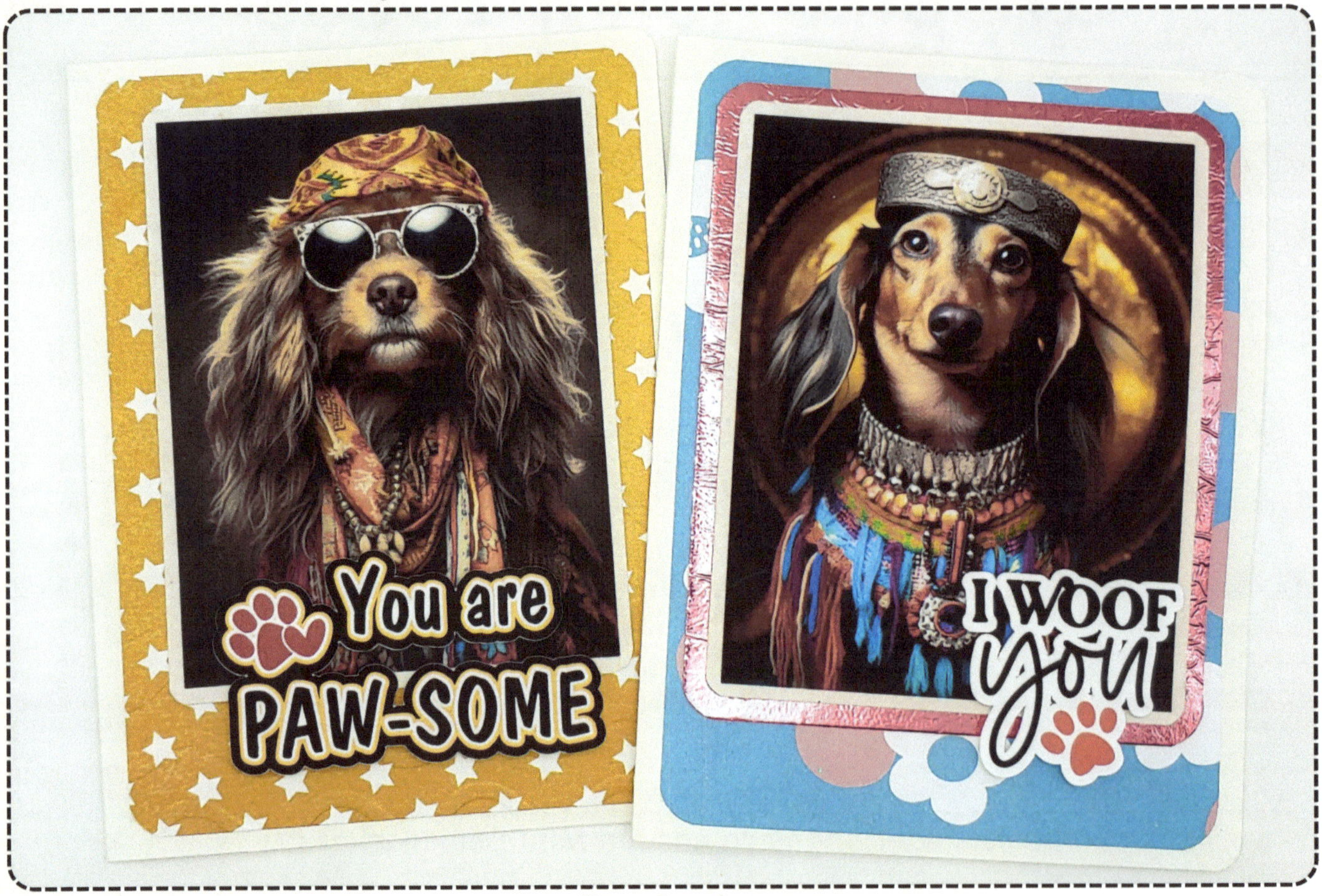

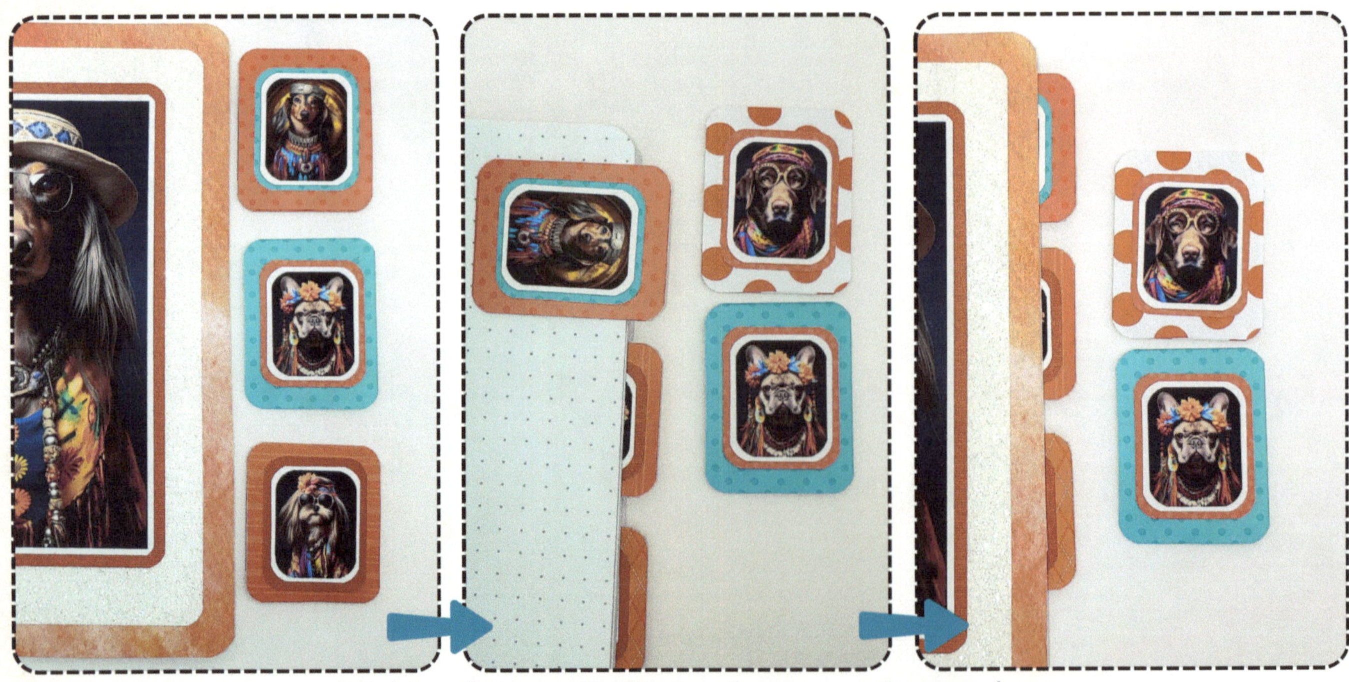

Fun Cards

Hidden Paperclip Tabs for your Journals

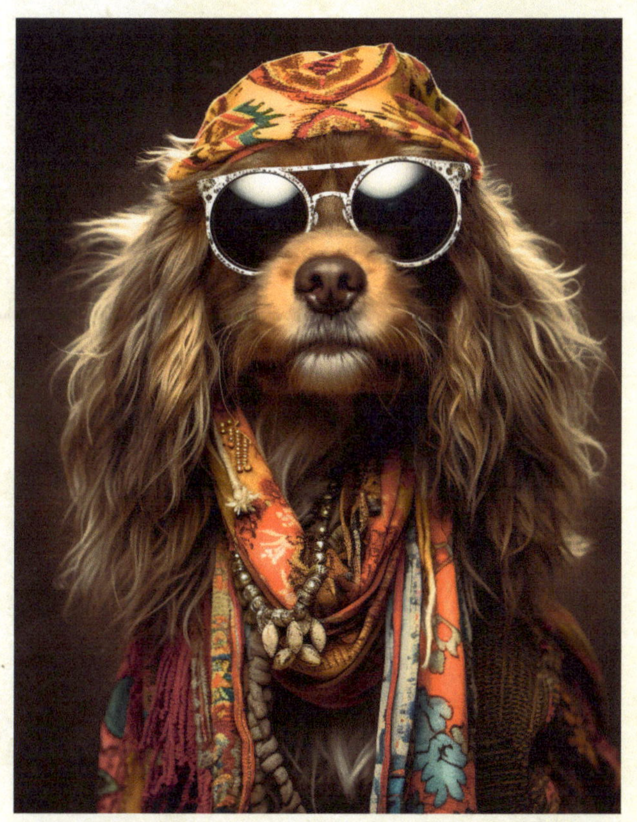

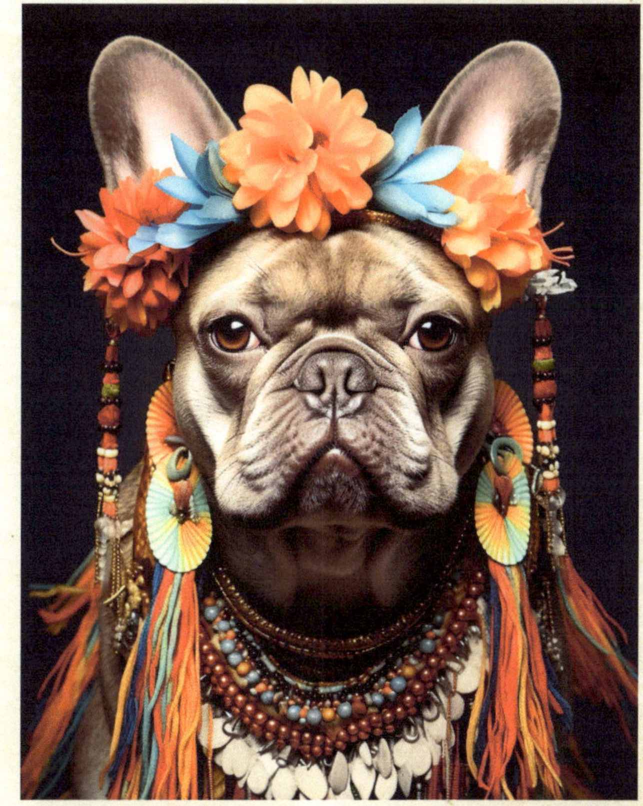

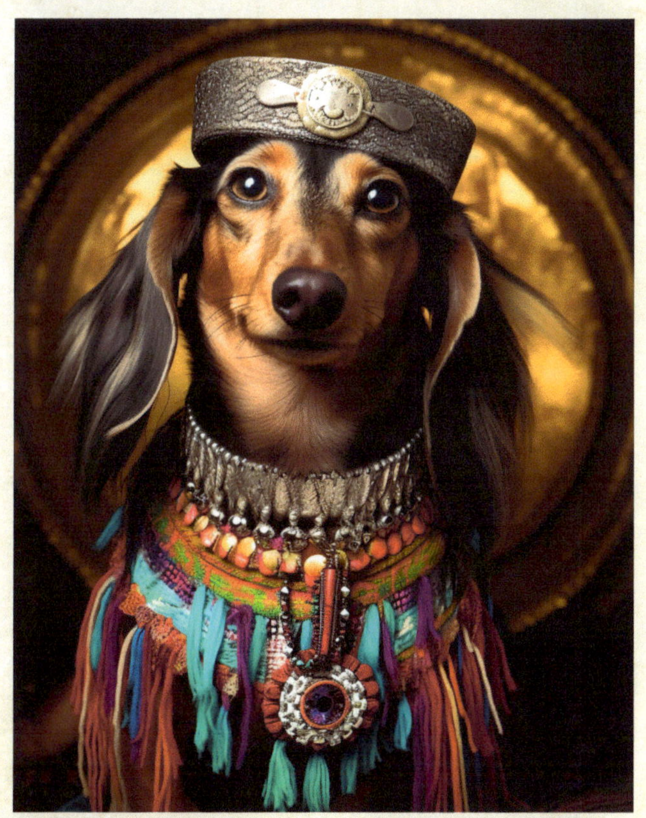

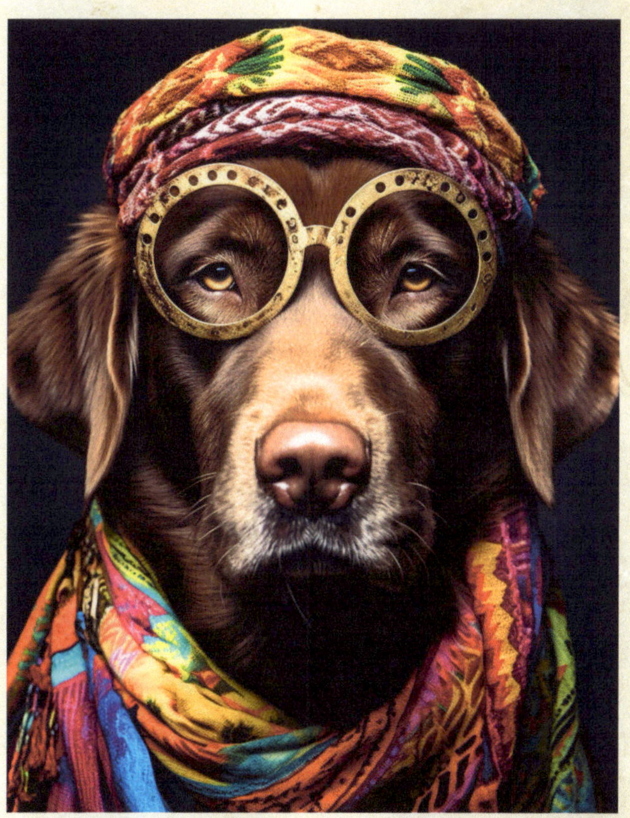

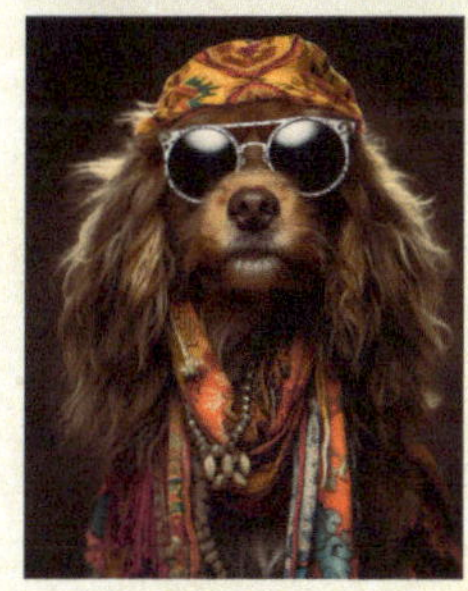

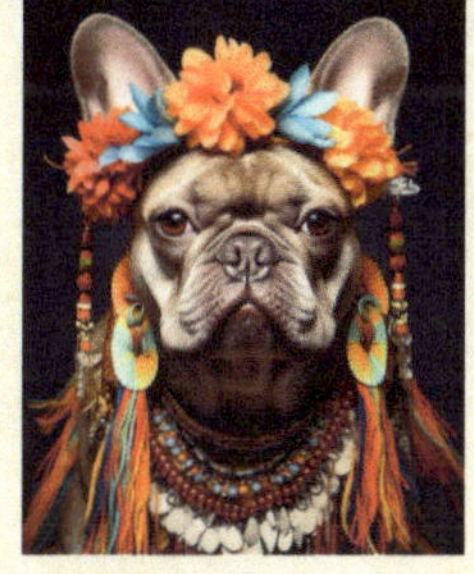

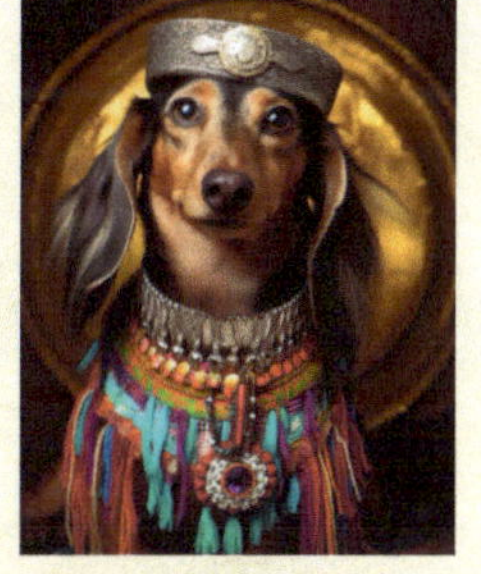

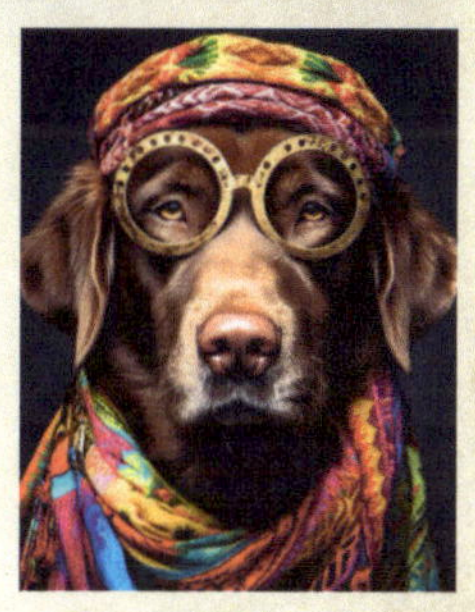

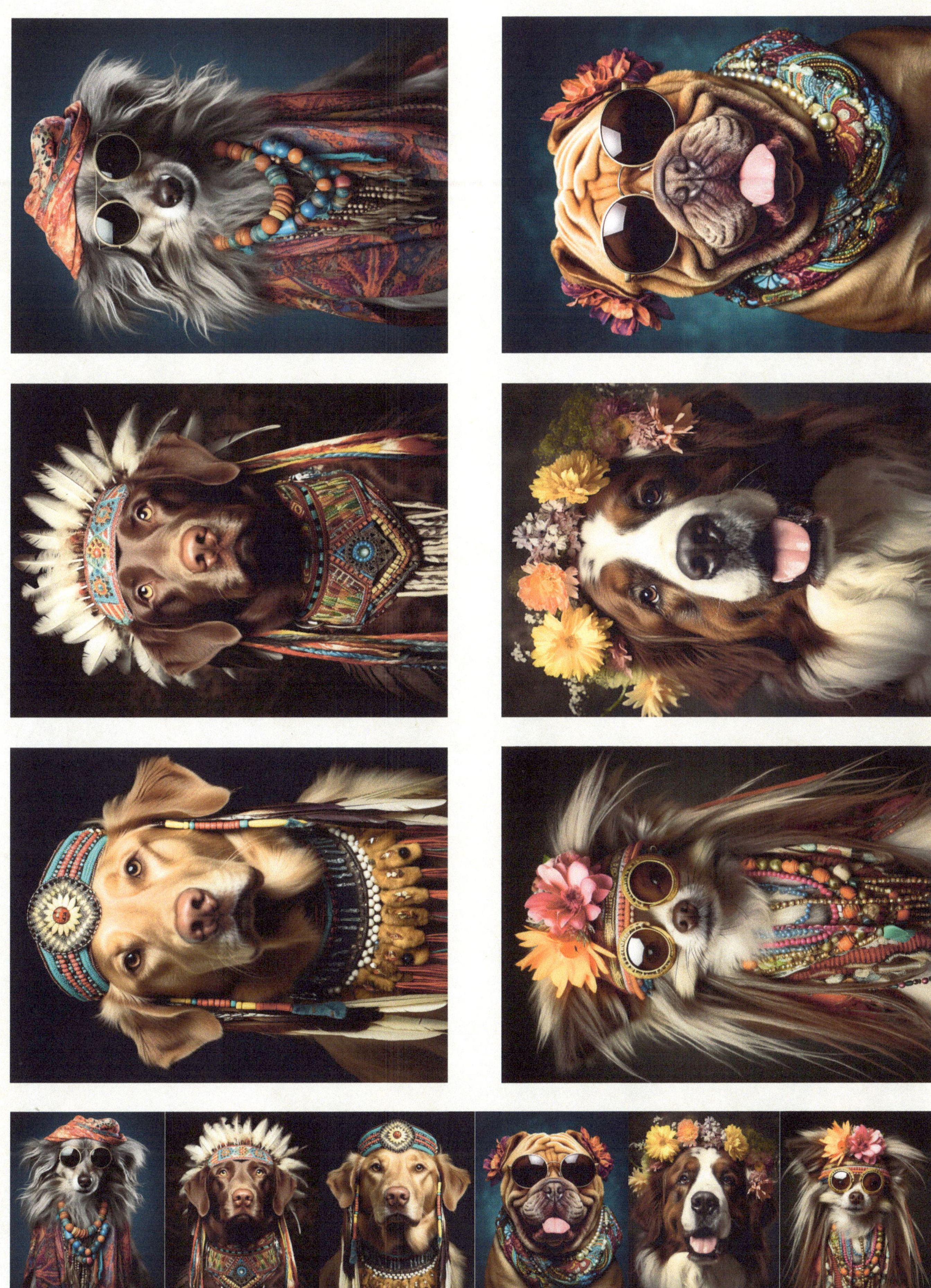

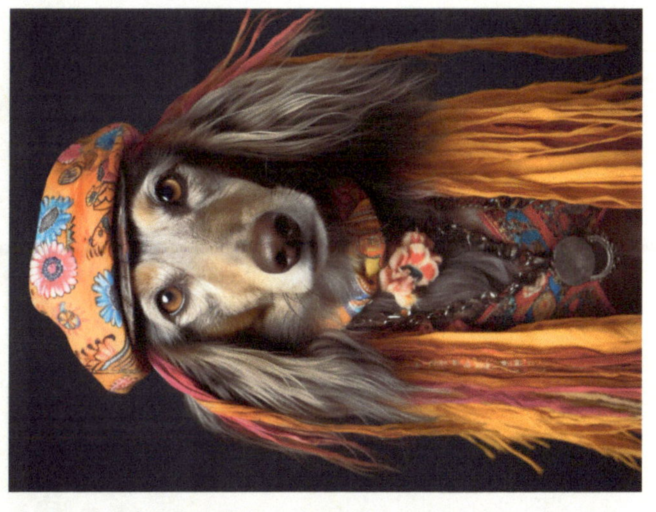
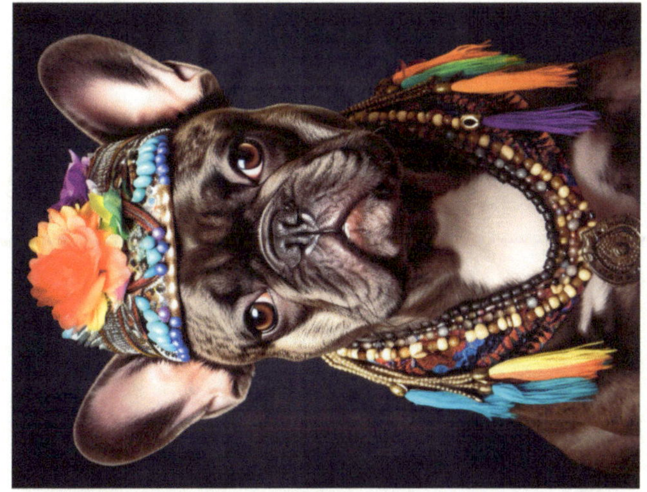
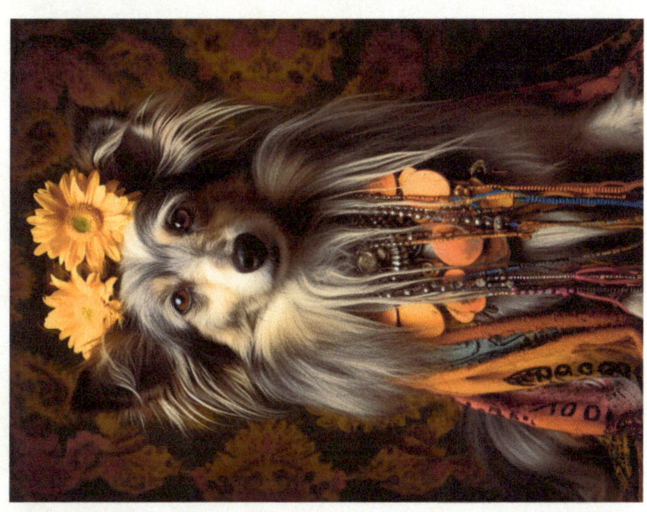
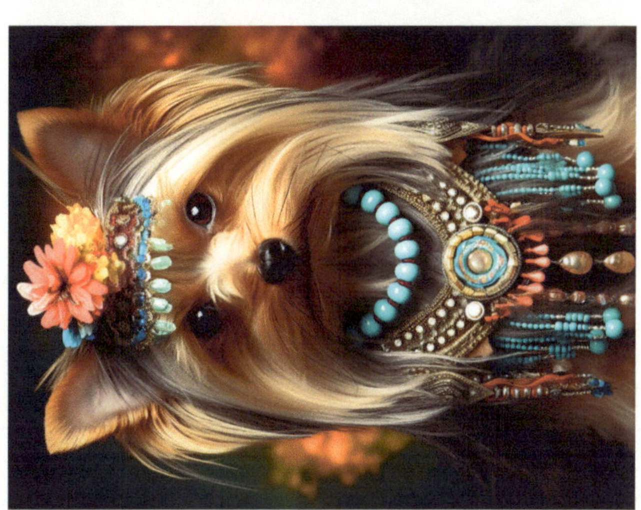
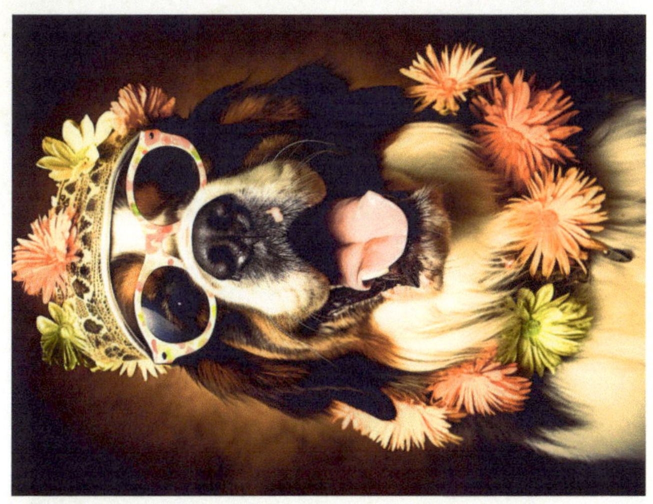
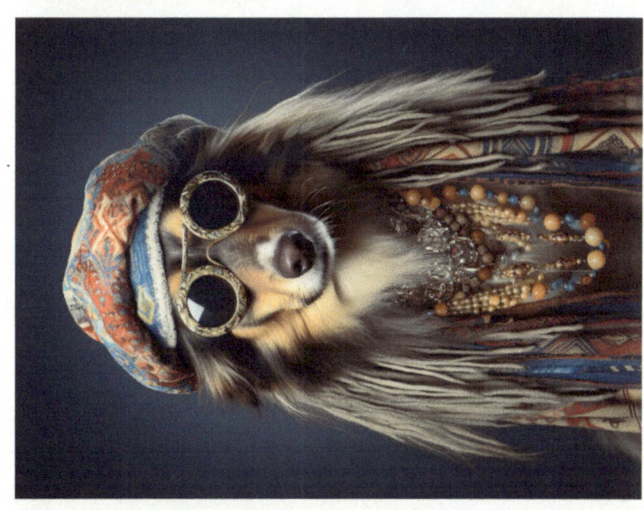
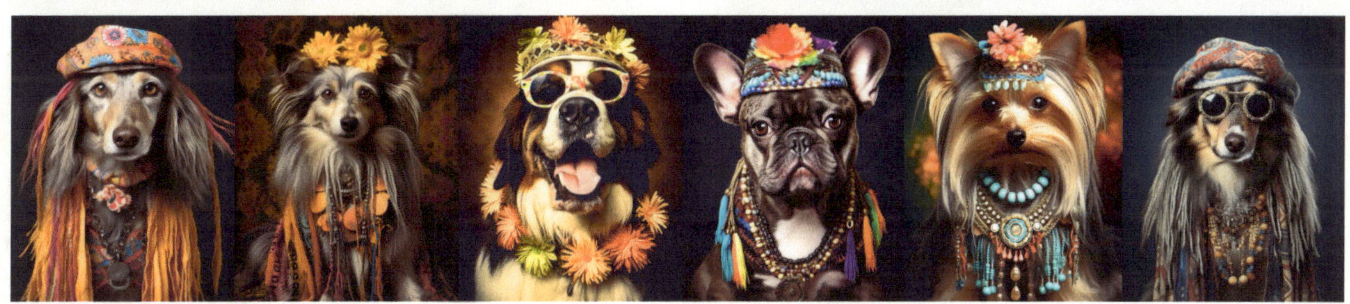

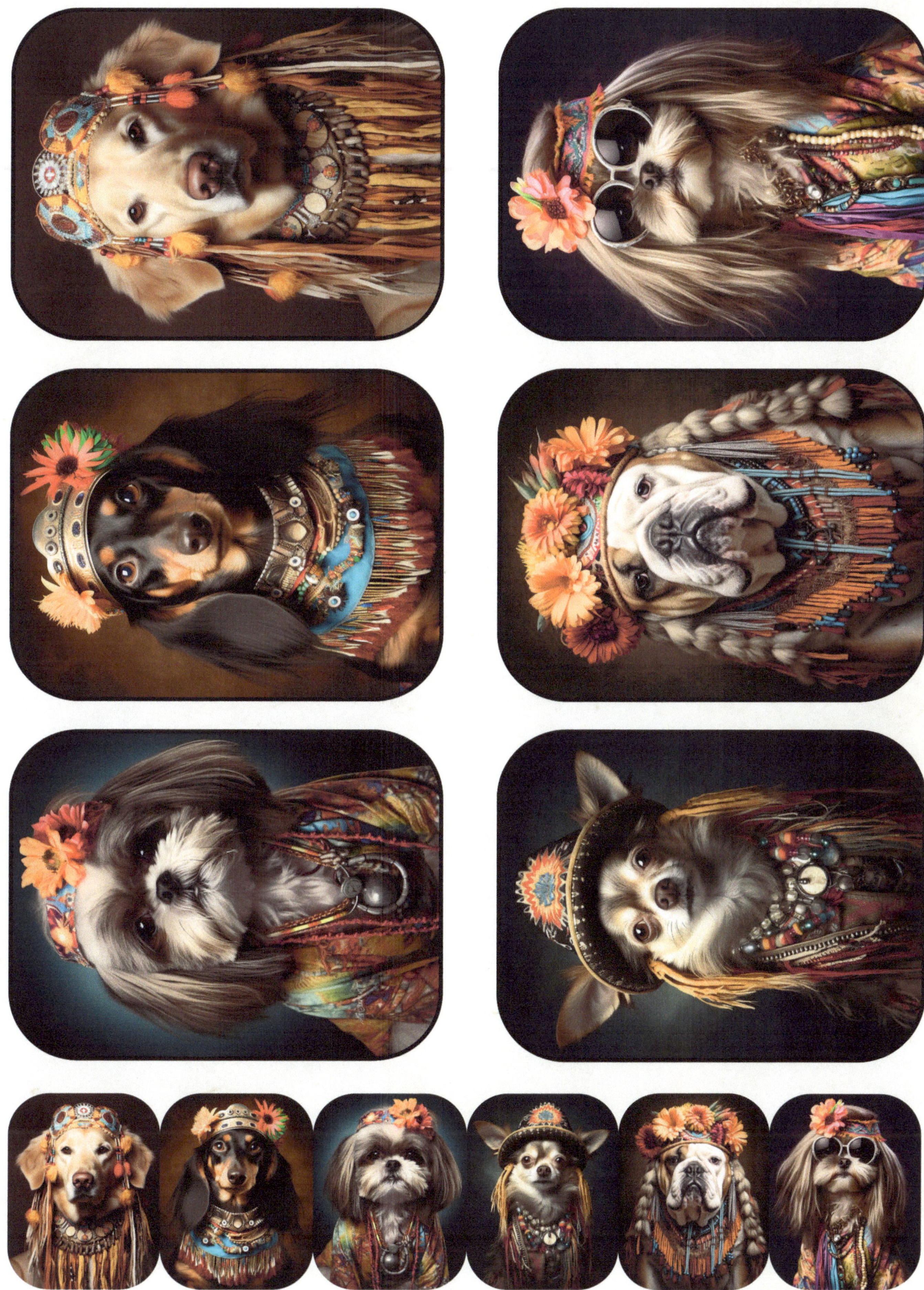

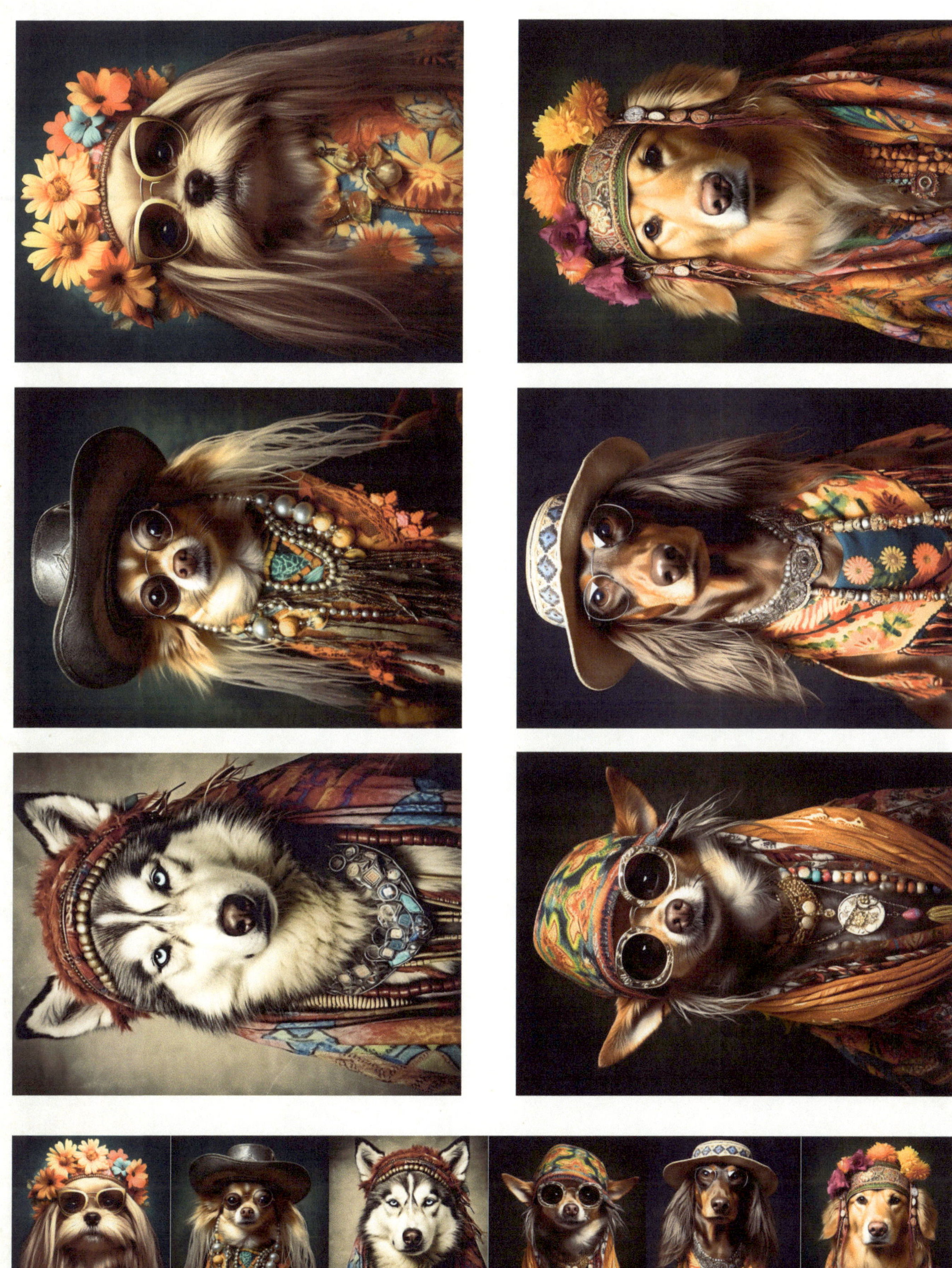

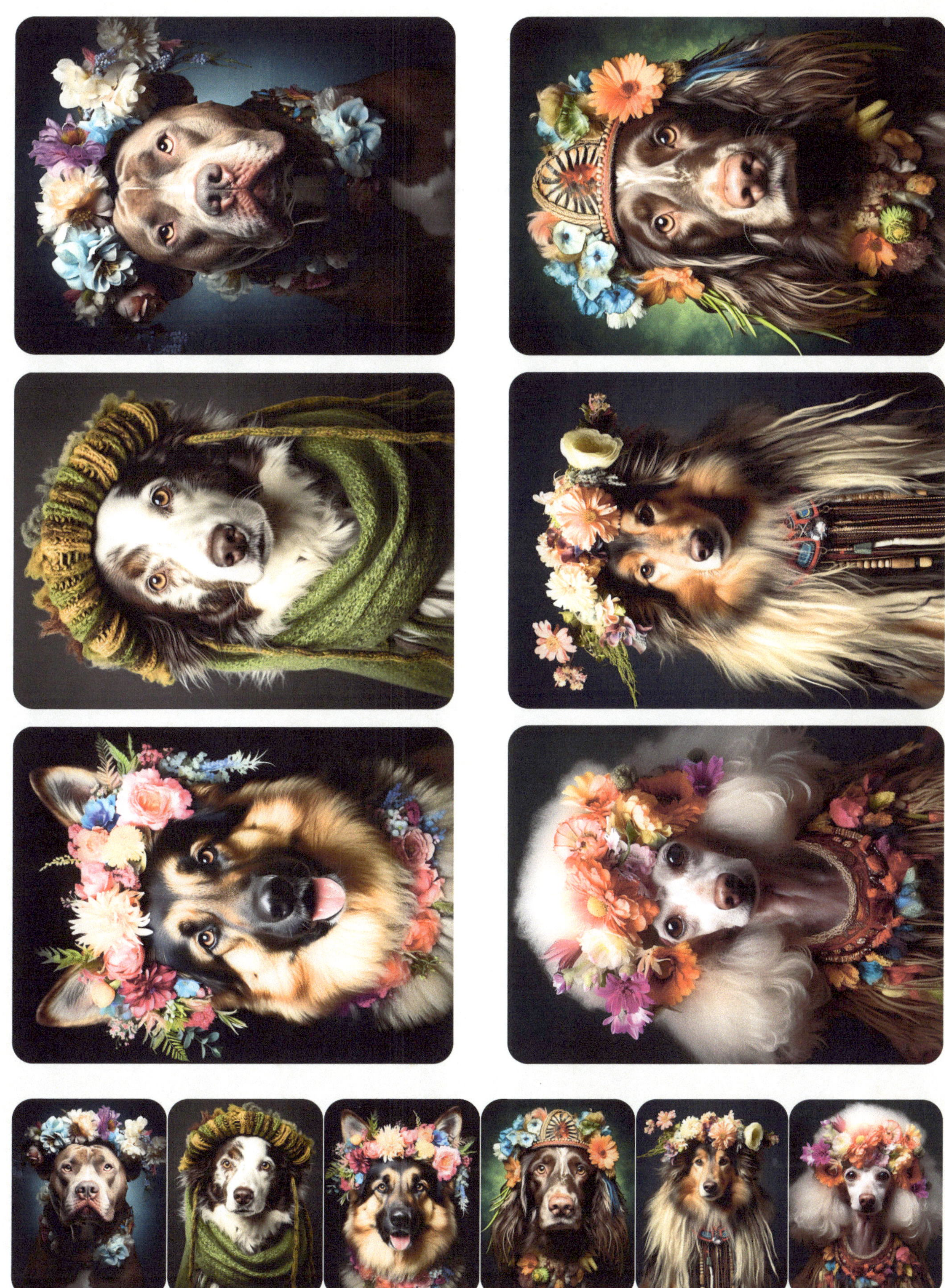

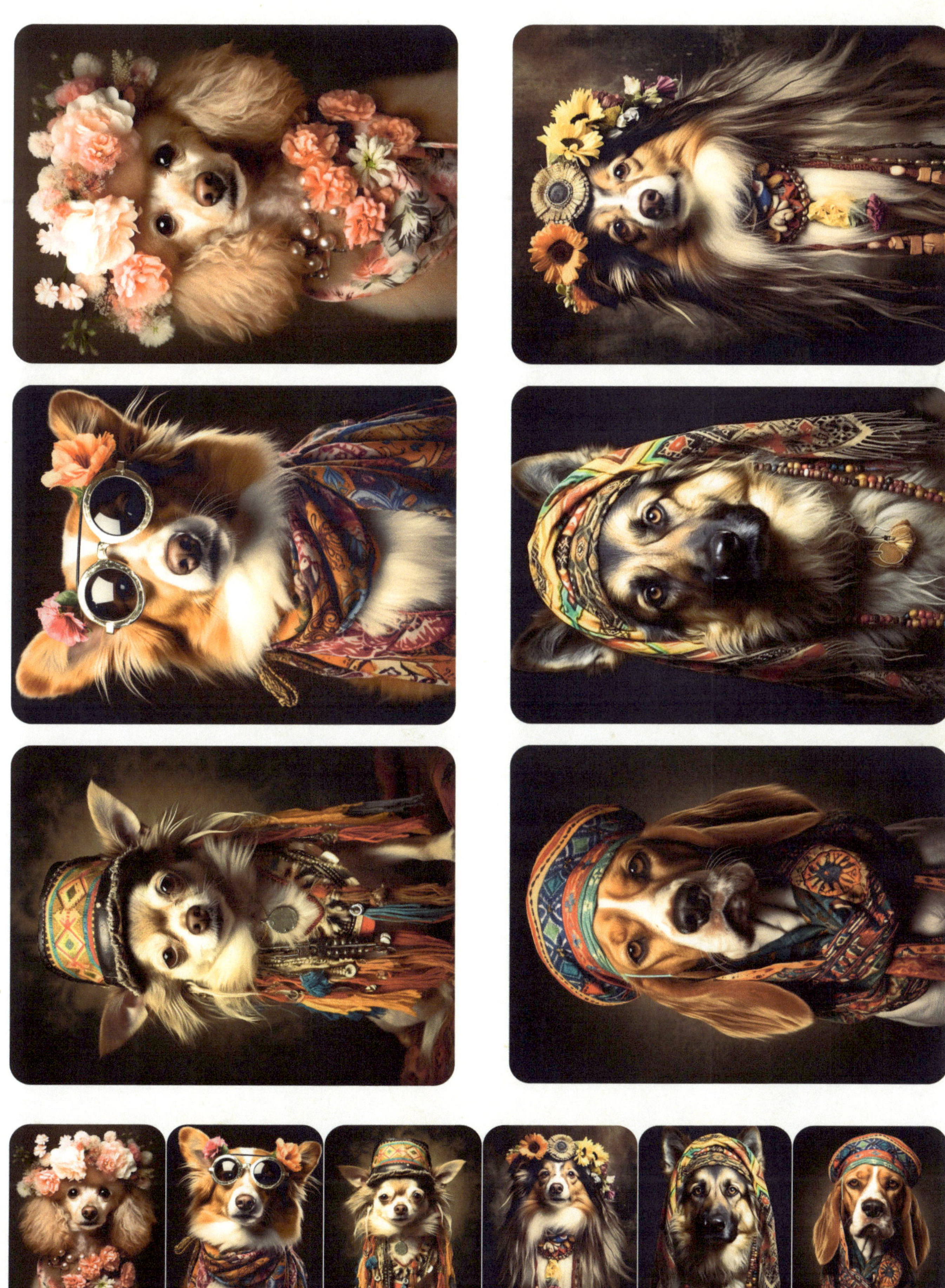

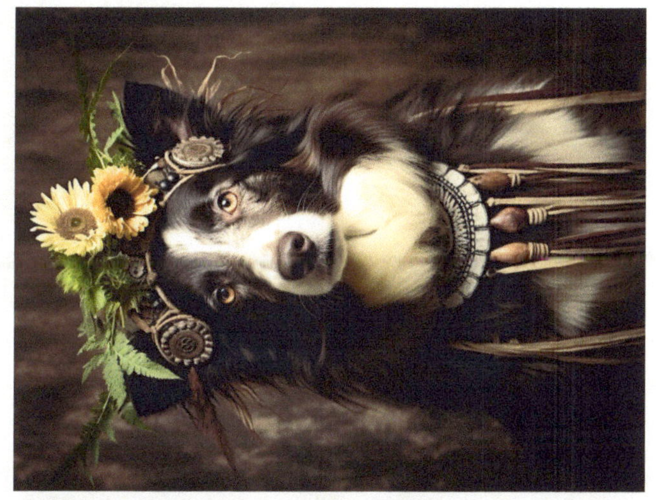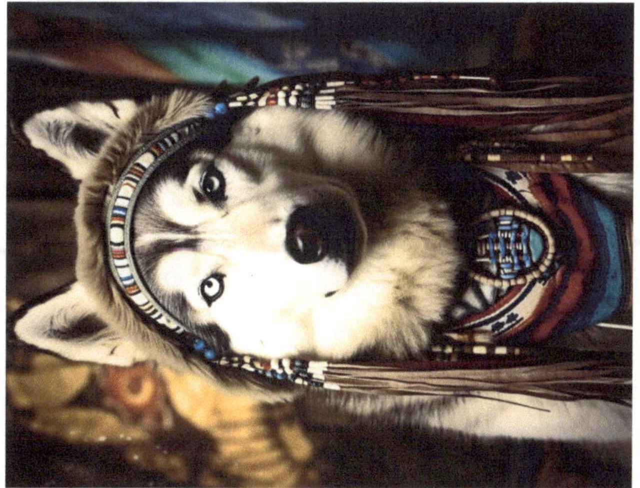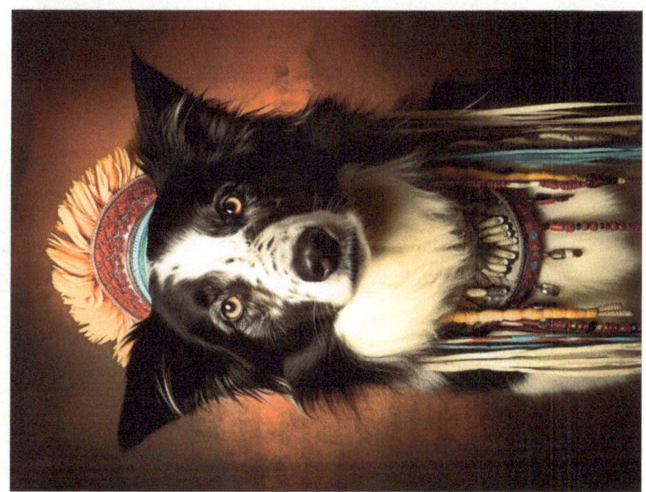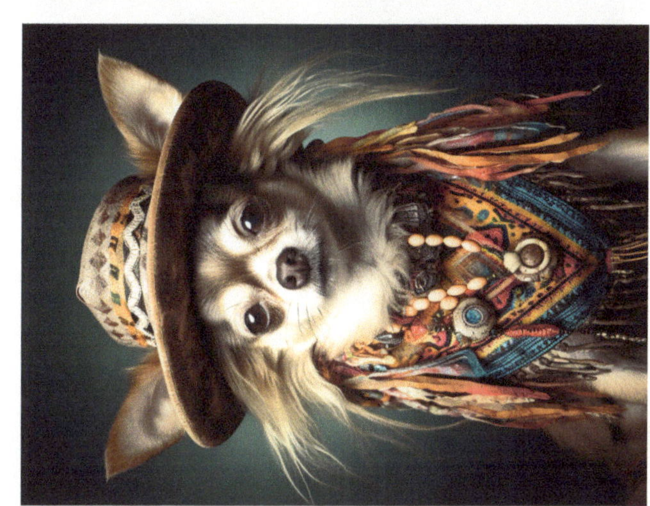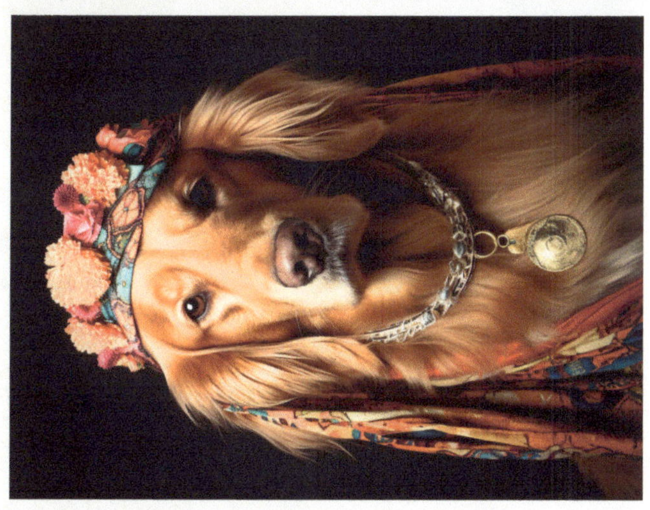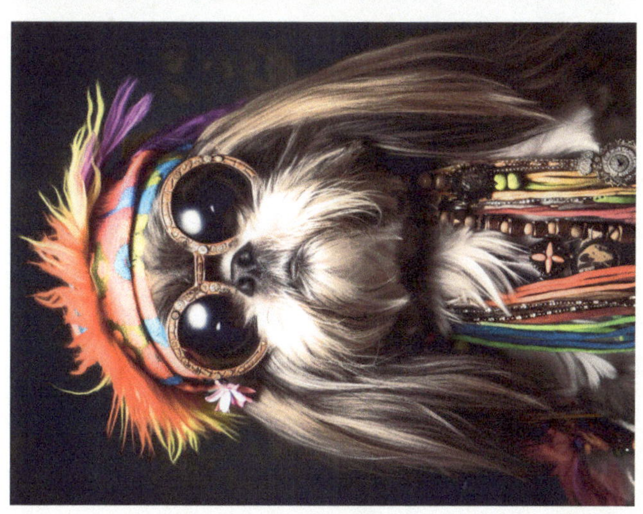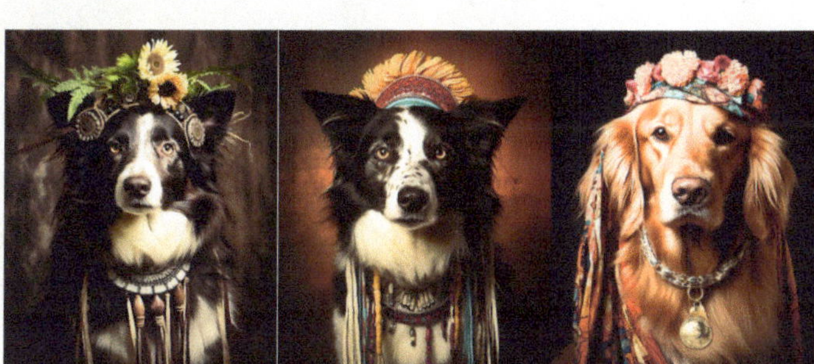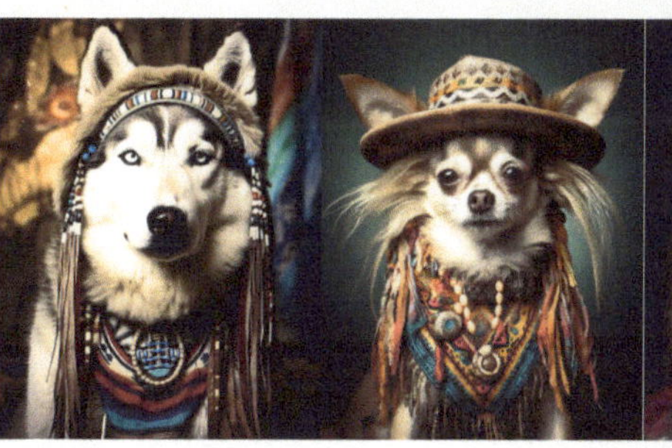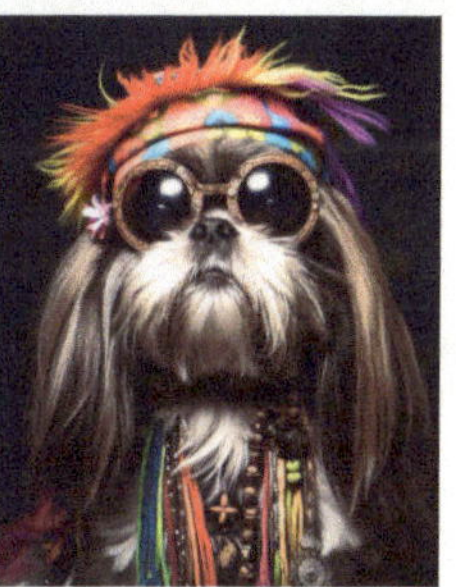

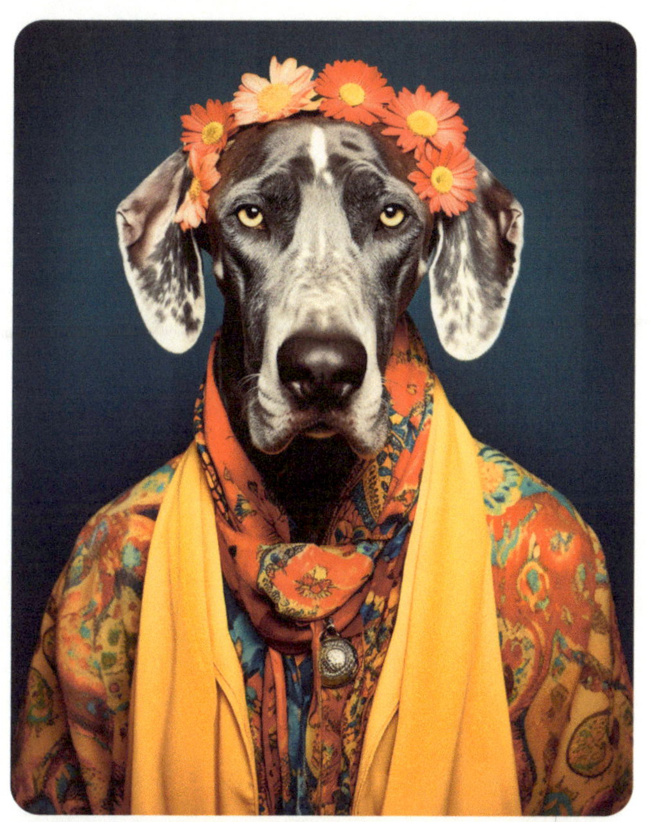
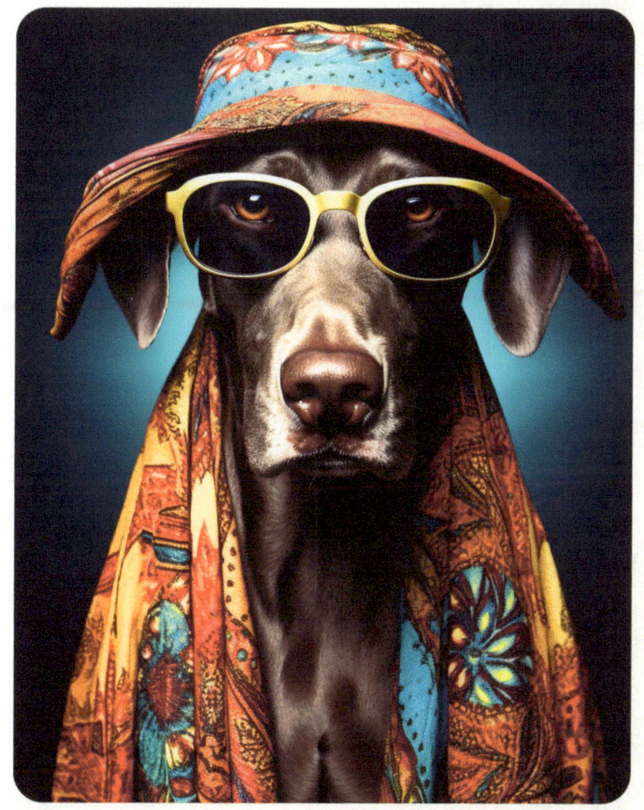
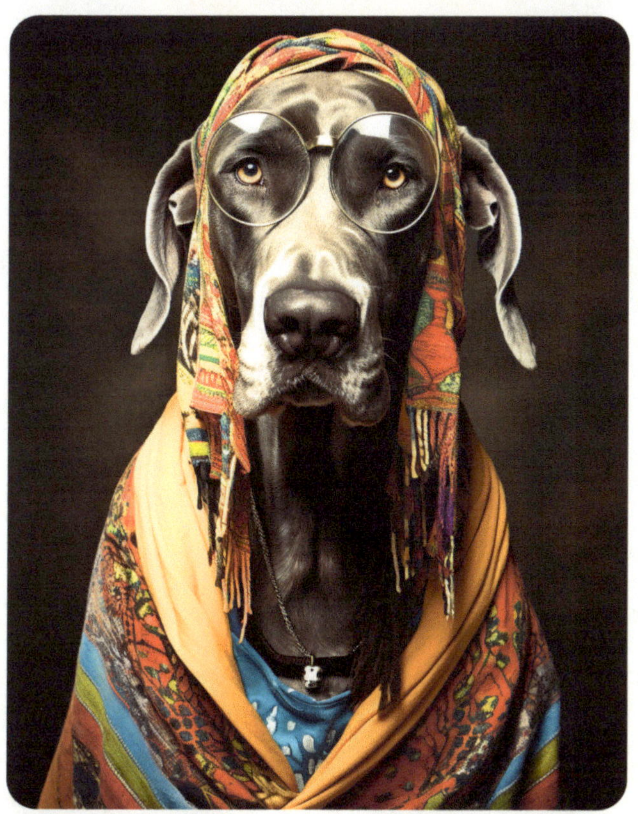
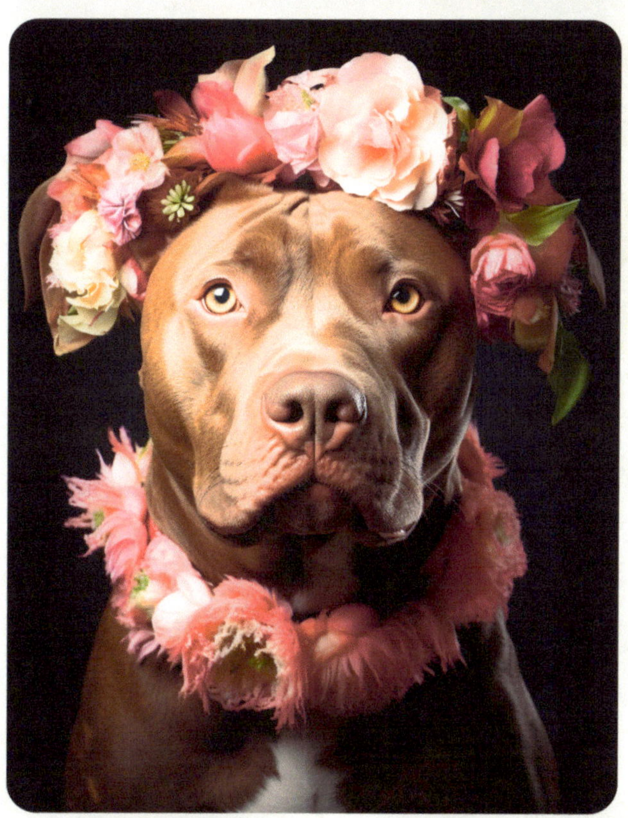
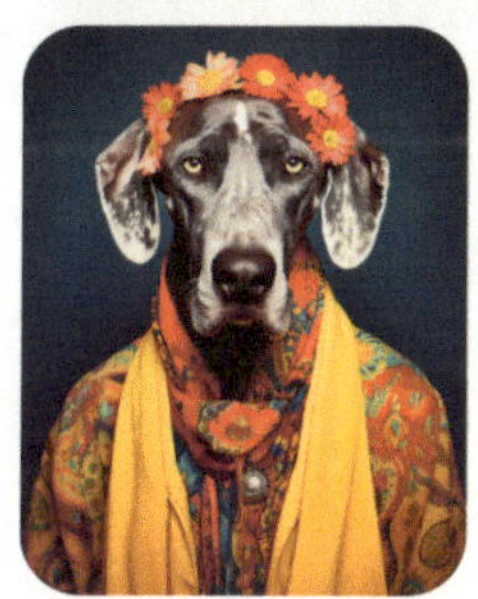
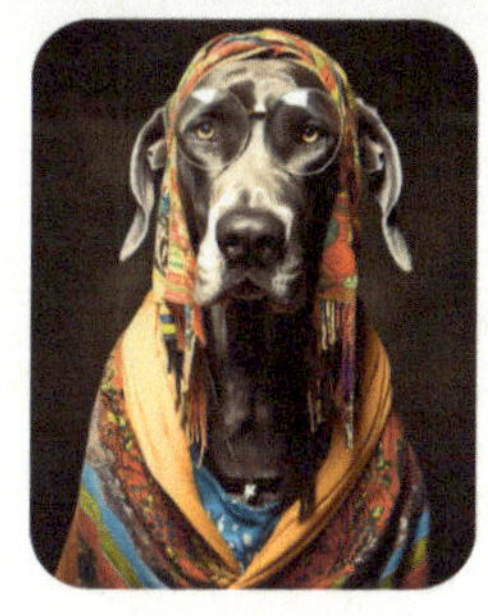
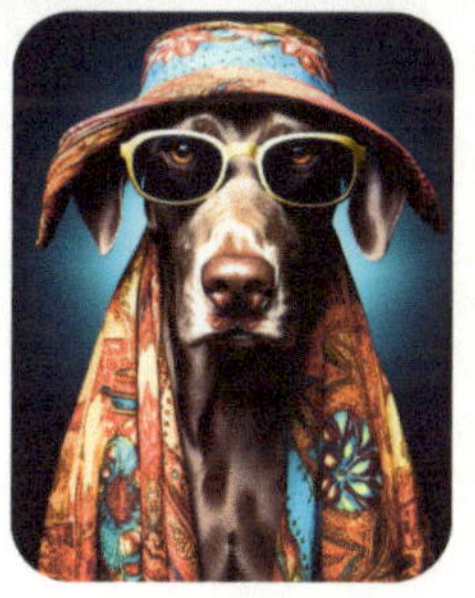
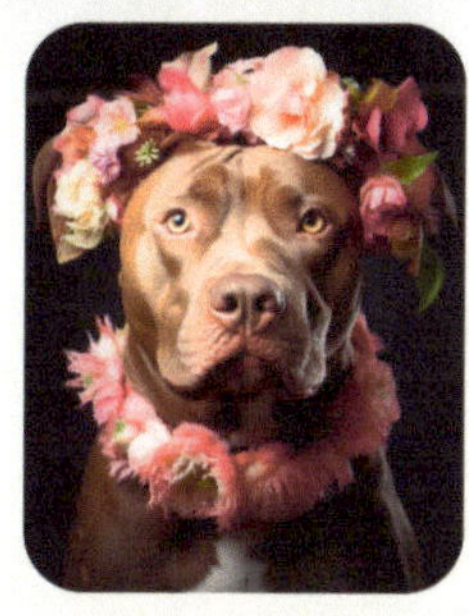

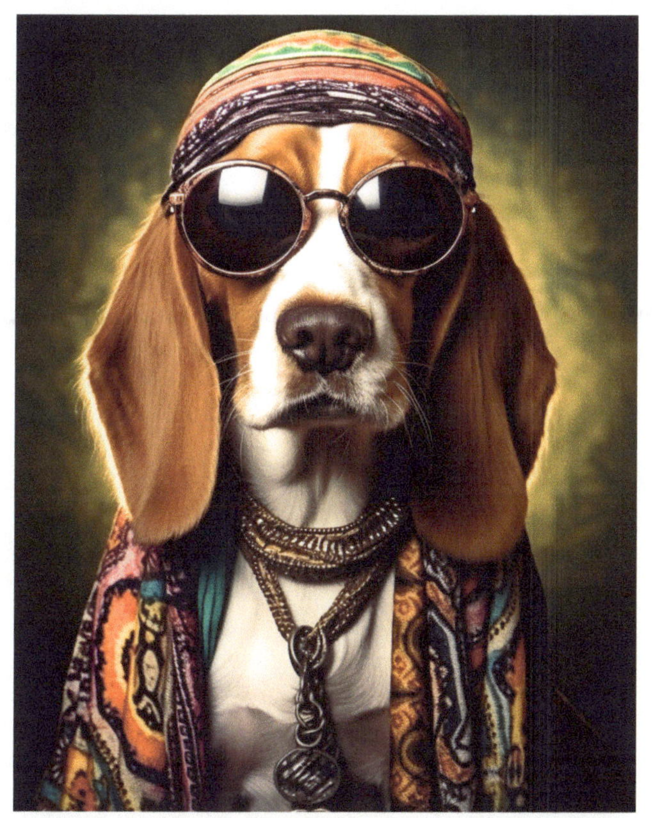
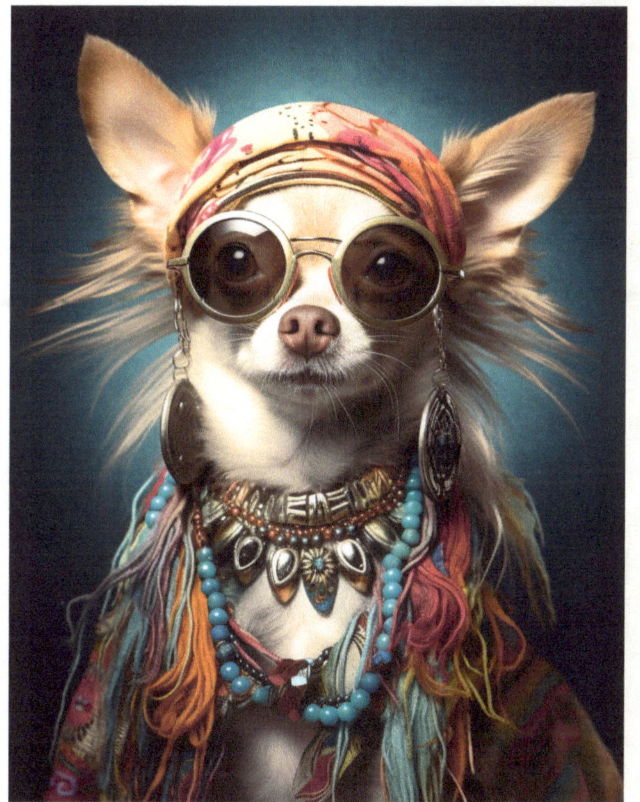
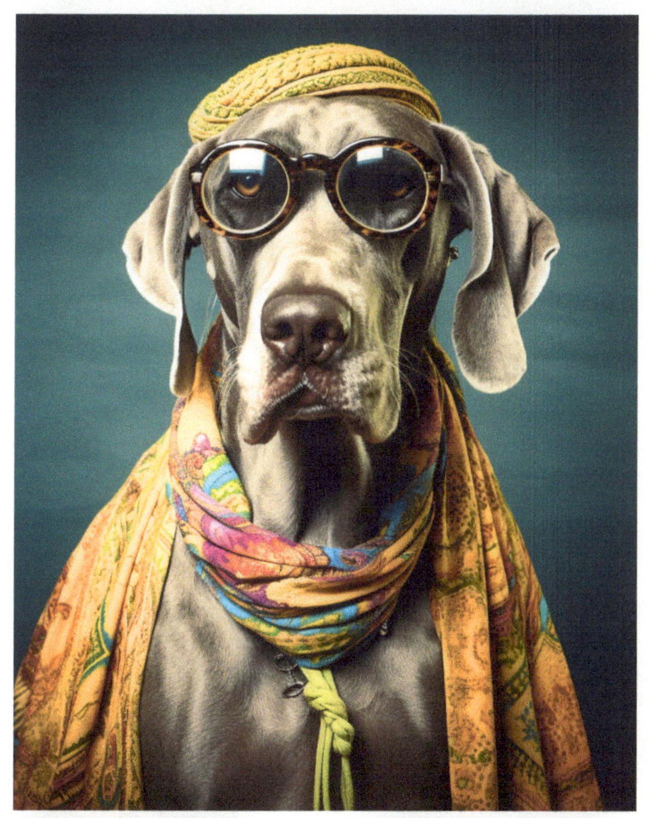
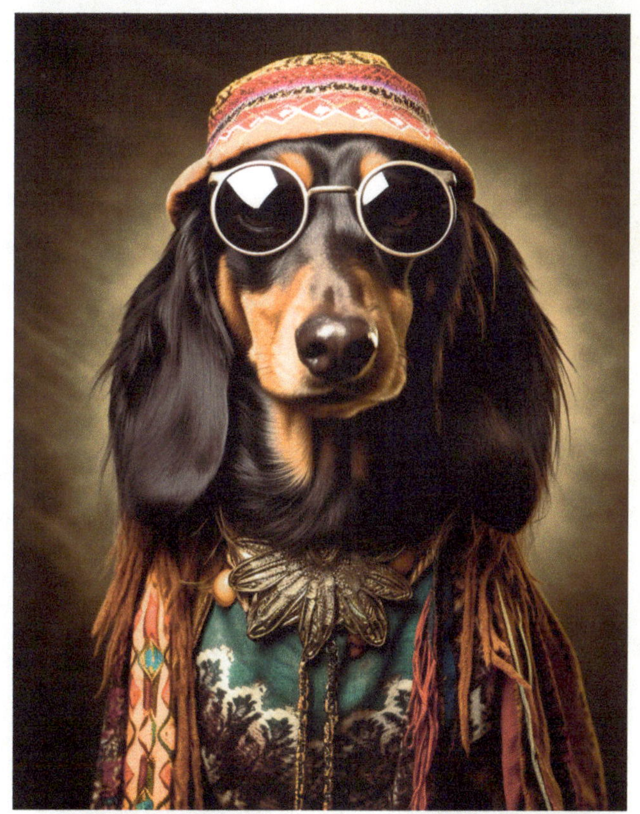
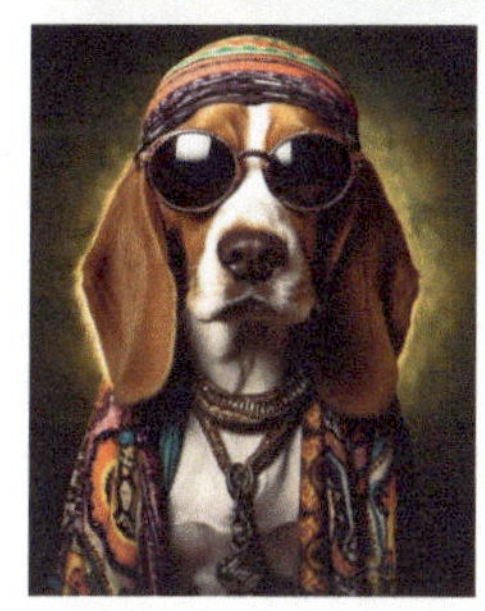
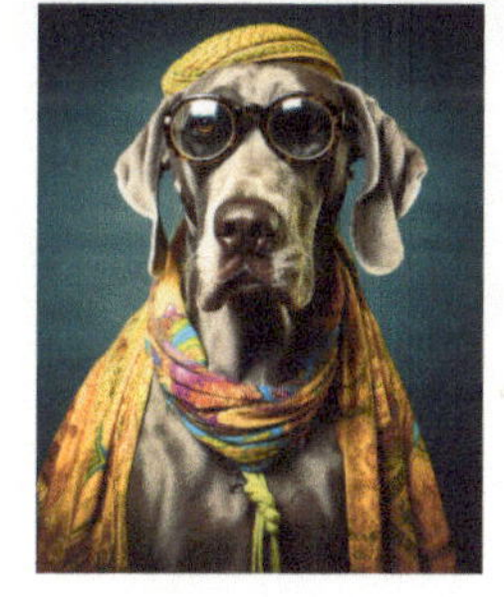
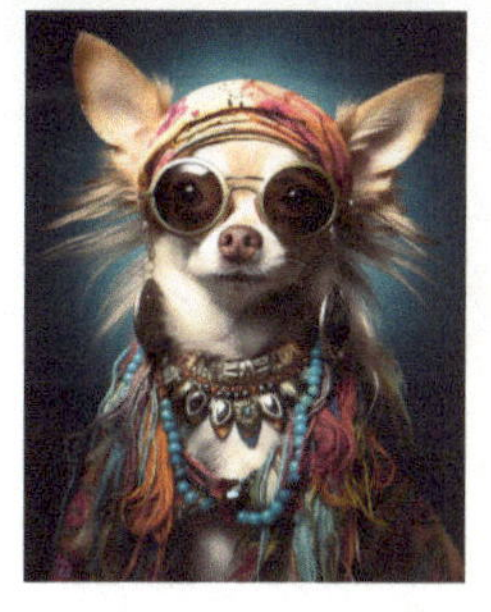
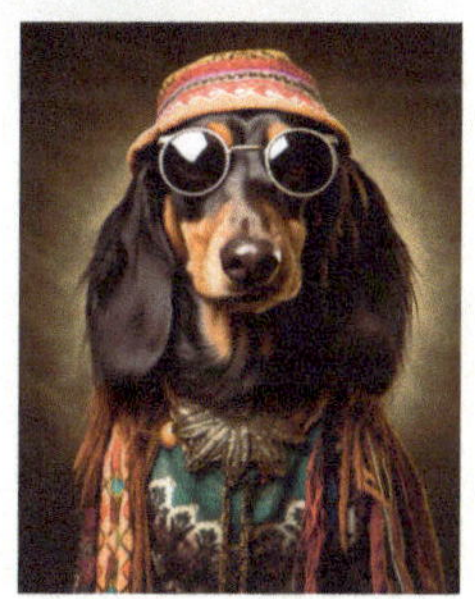

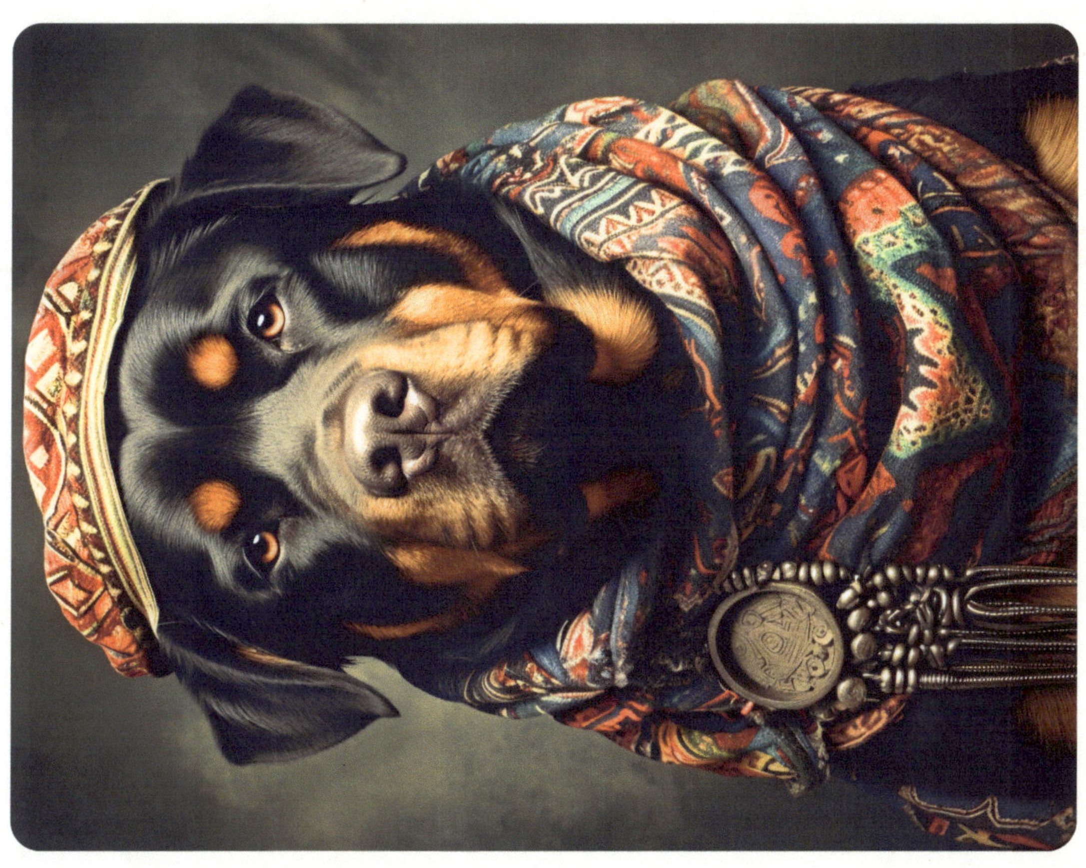
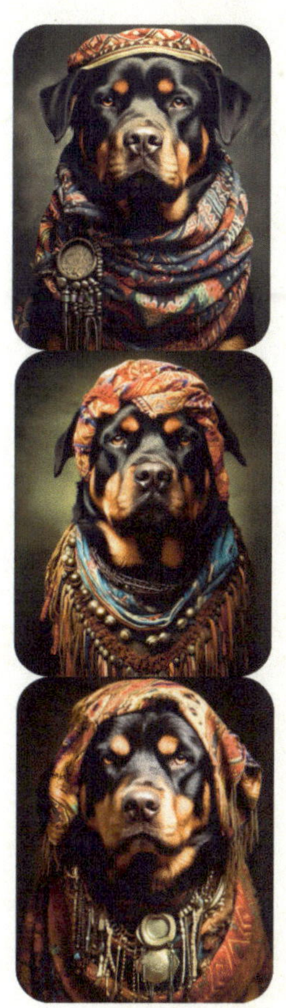
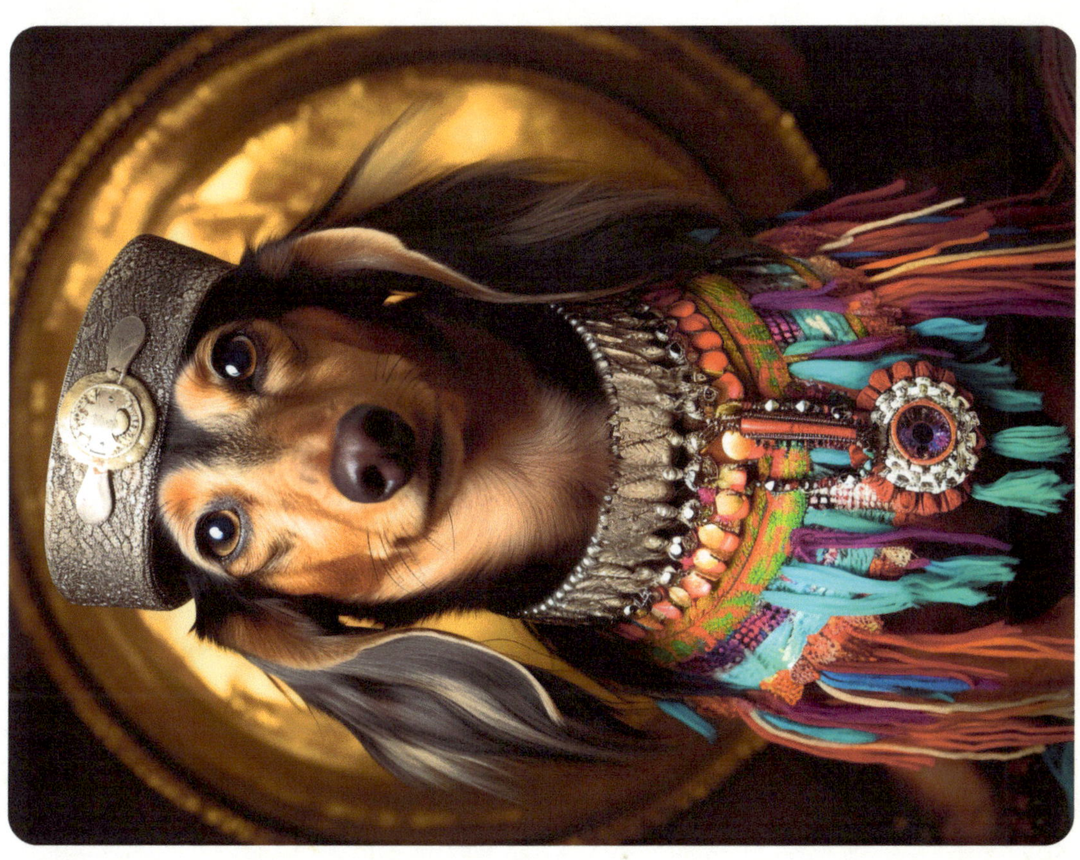
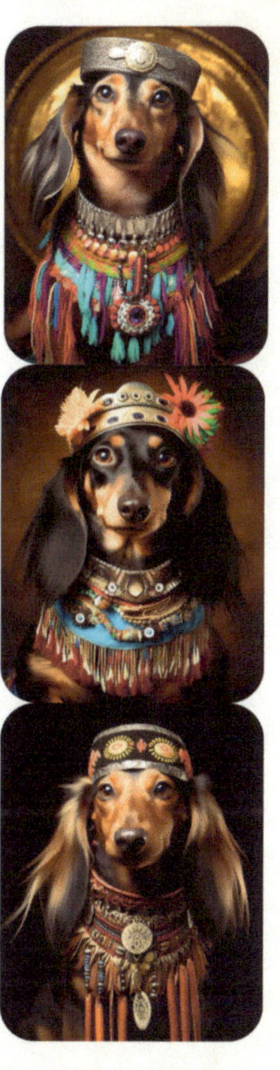

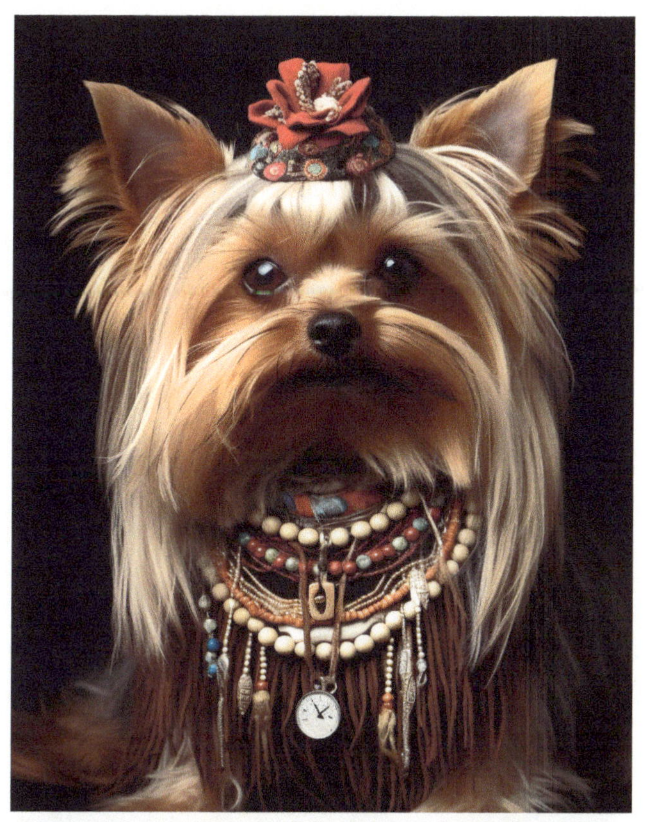
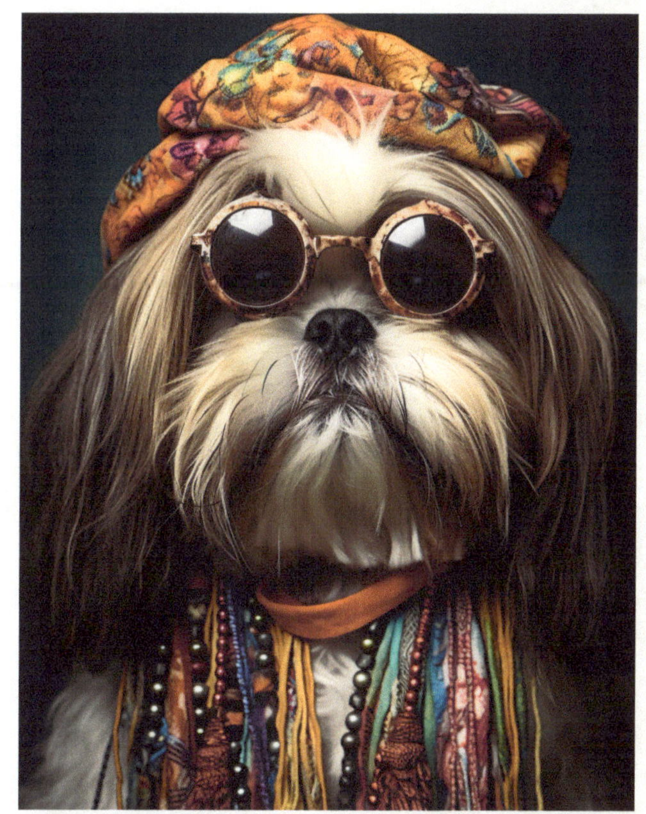
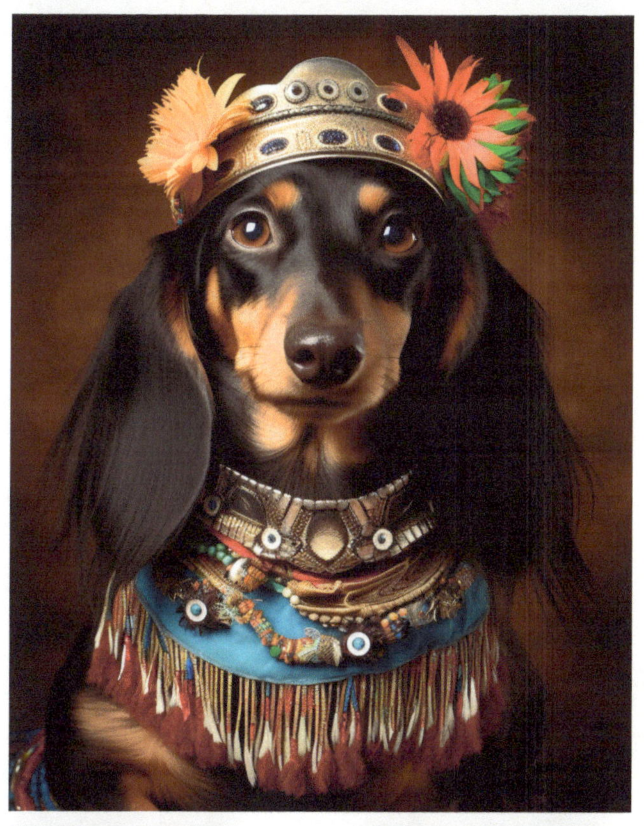
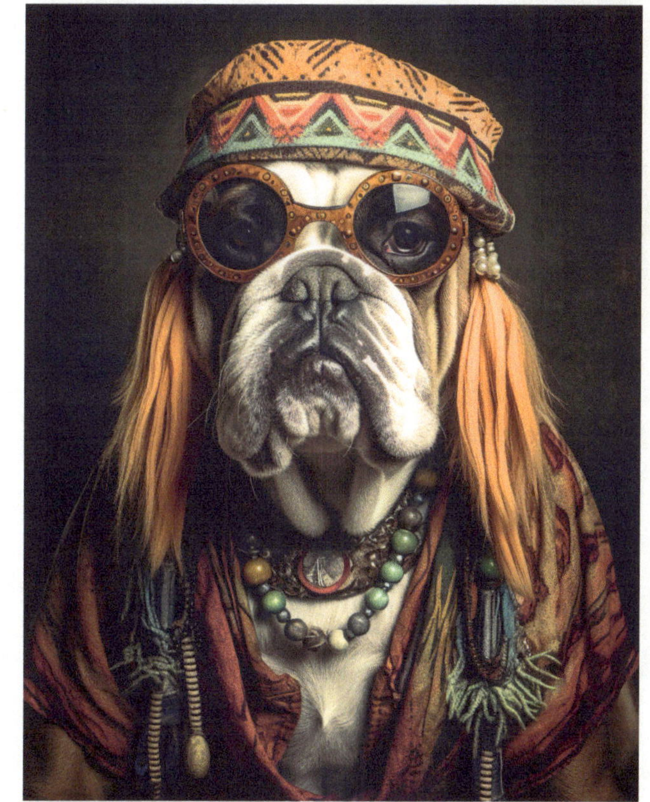
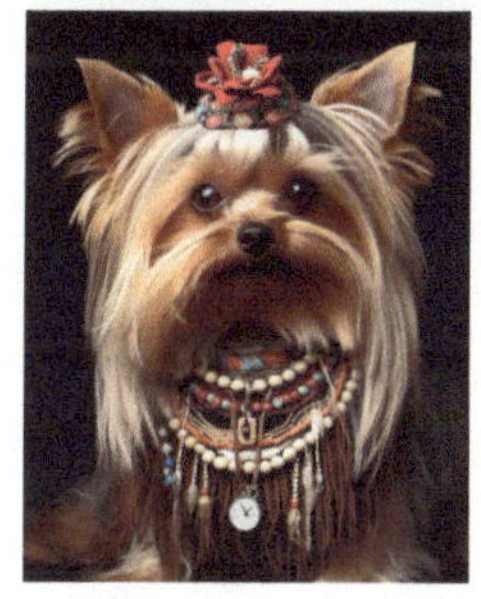
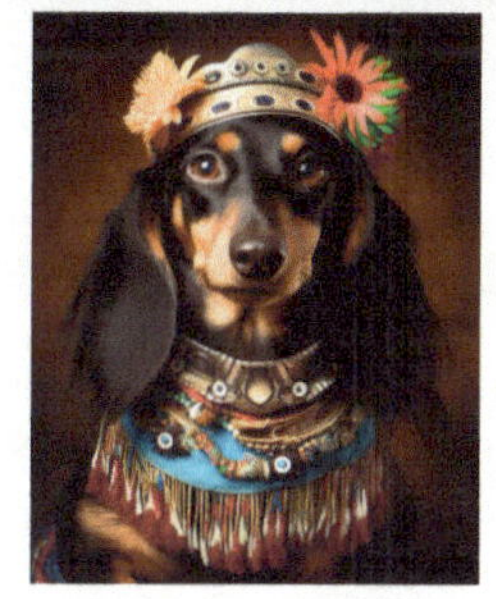
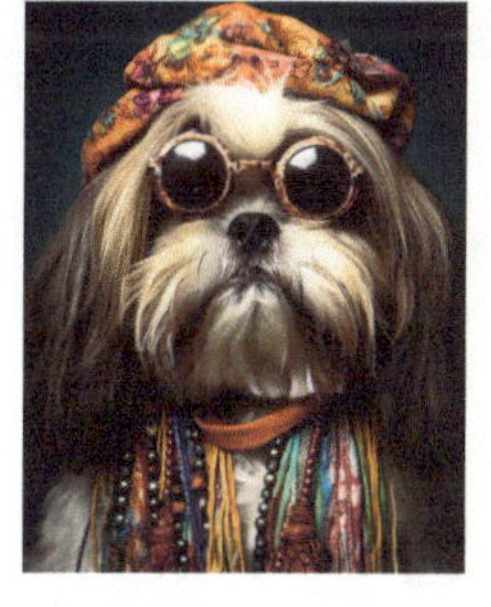
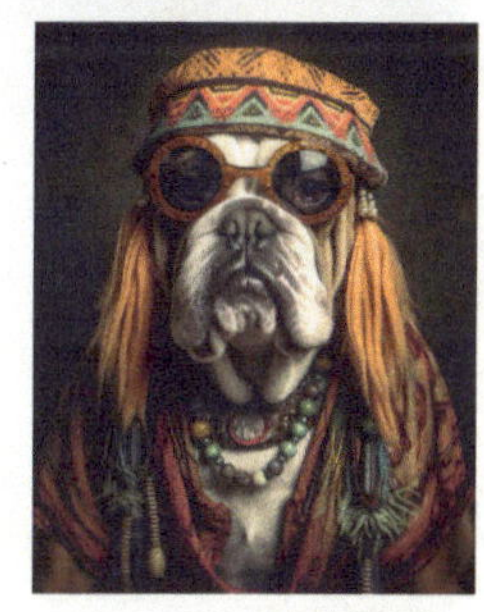

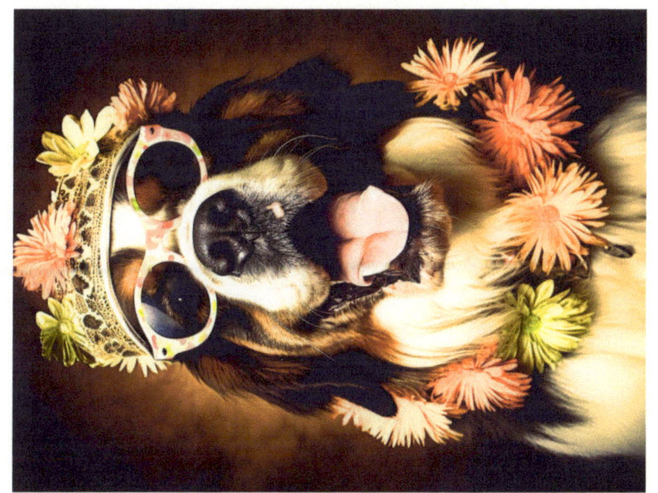
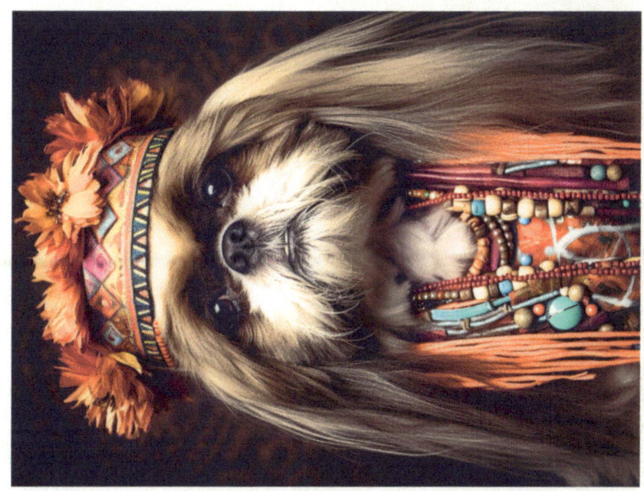
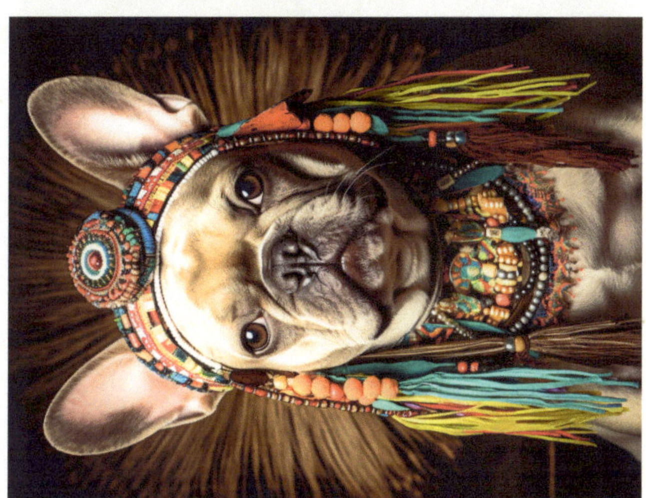
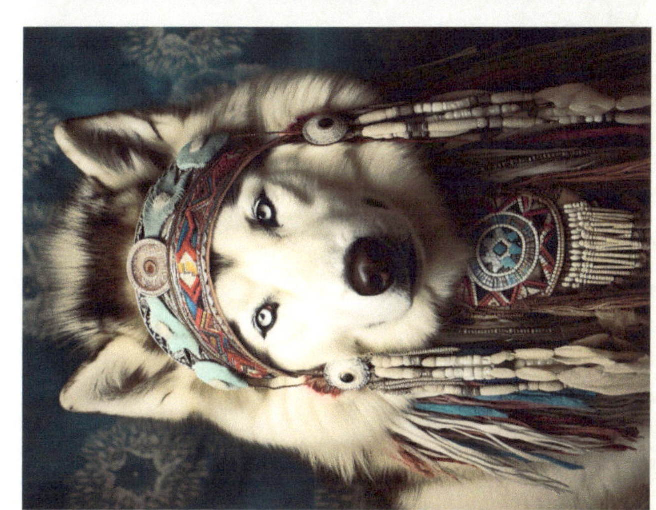
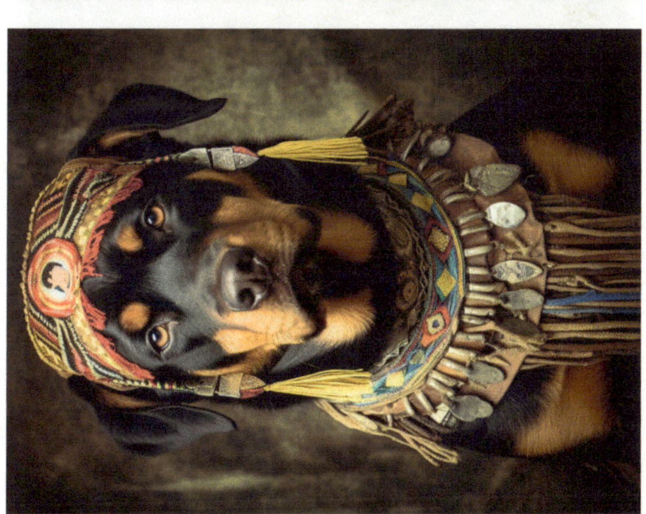
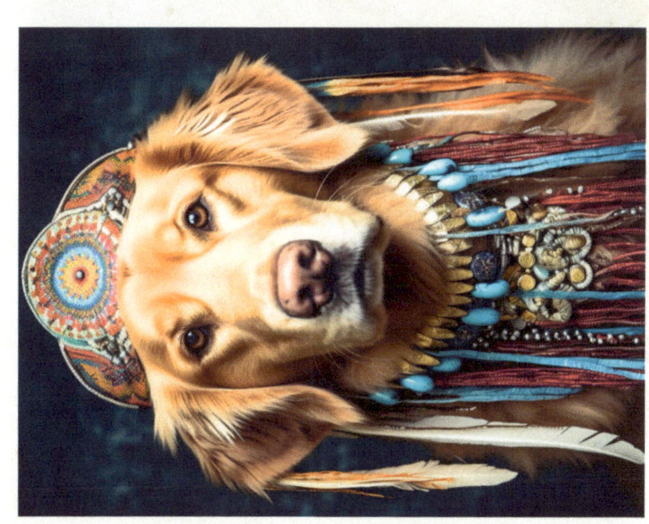
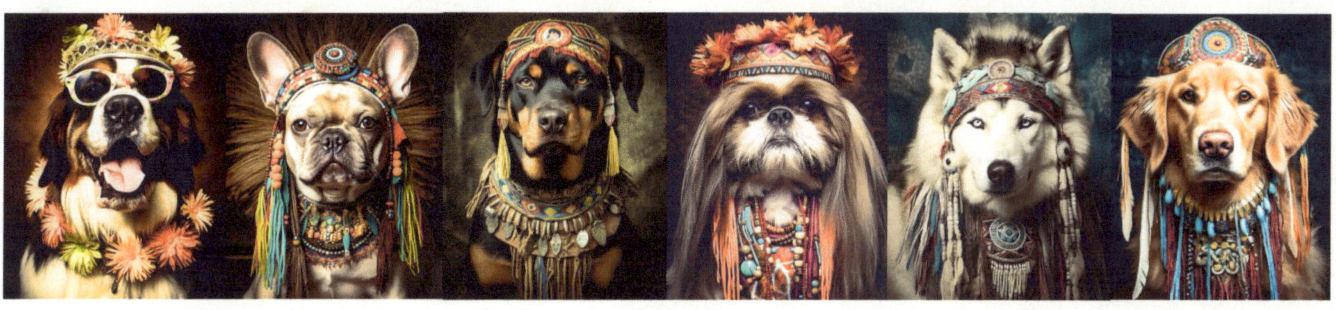

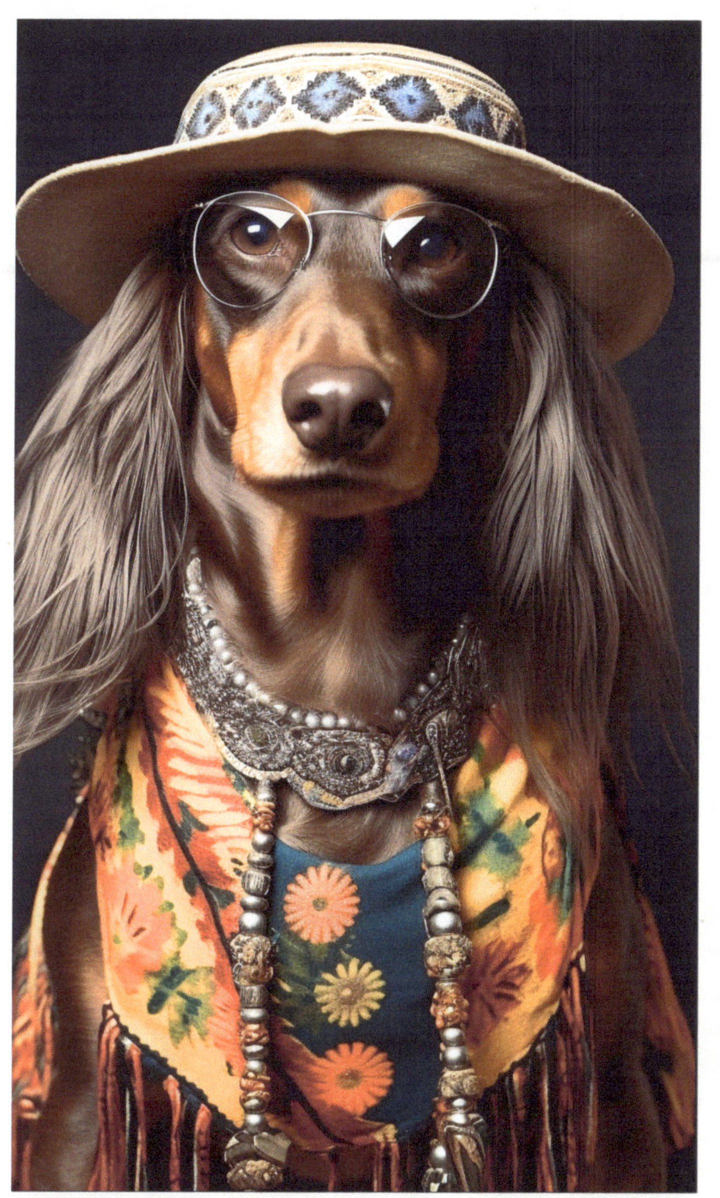
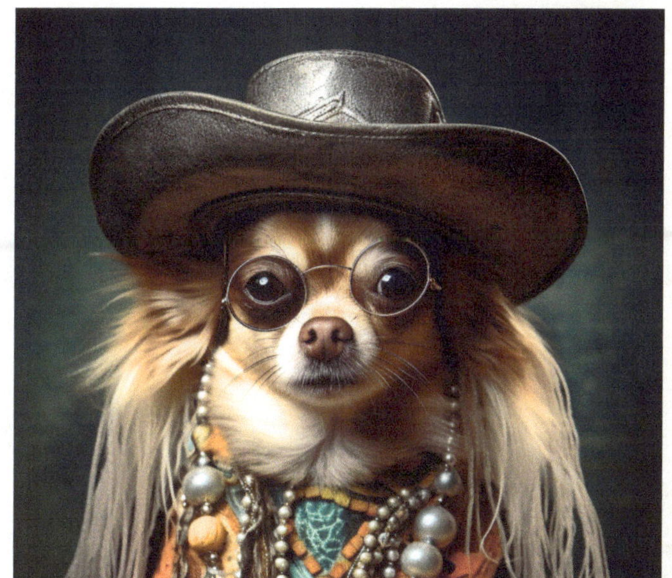
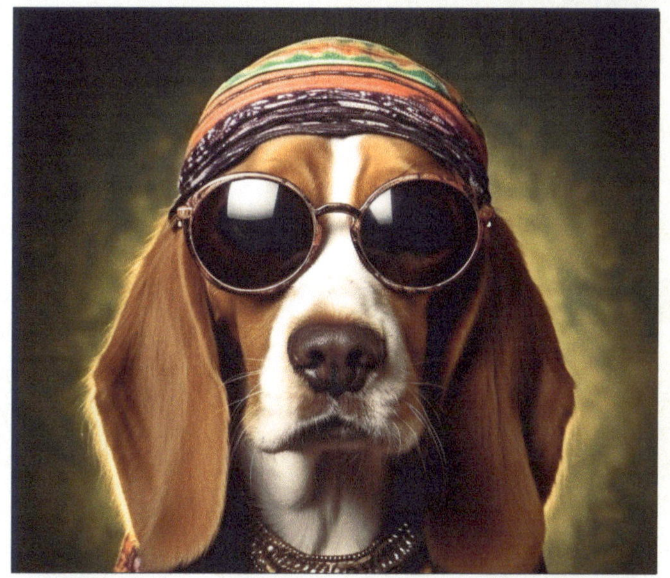
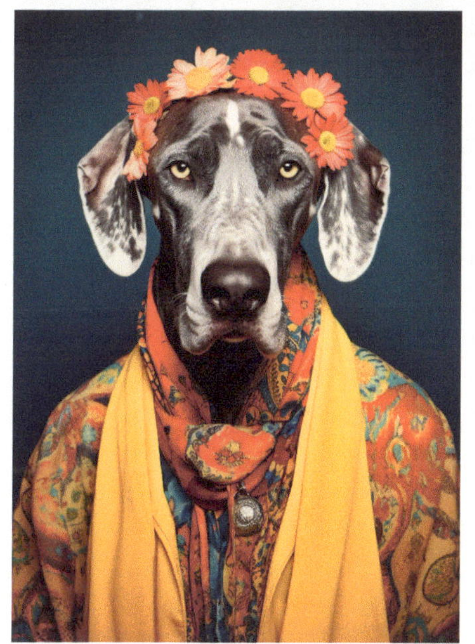
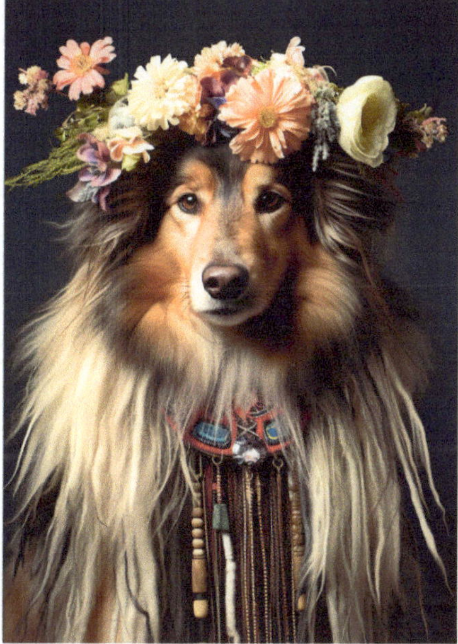
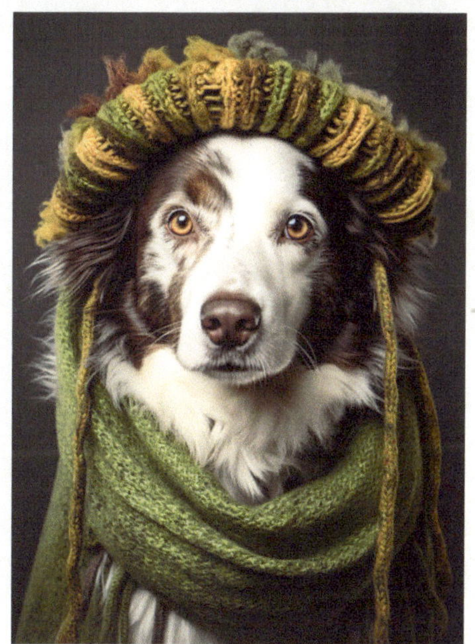

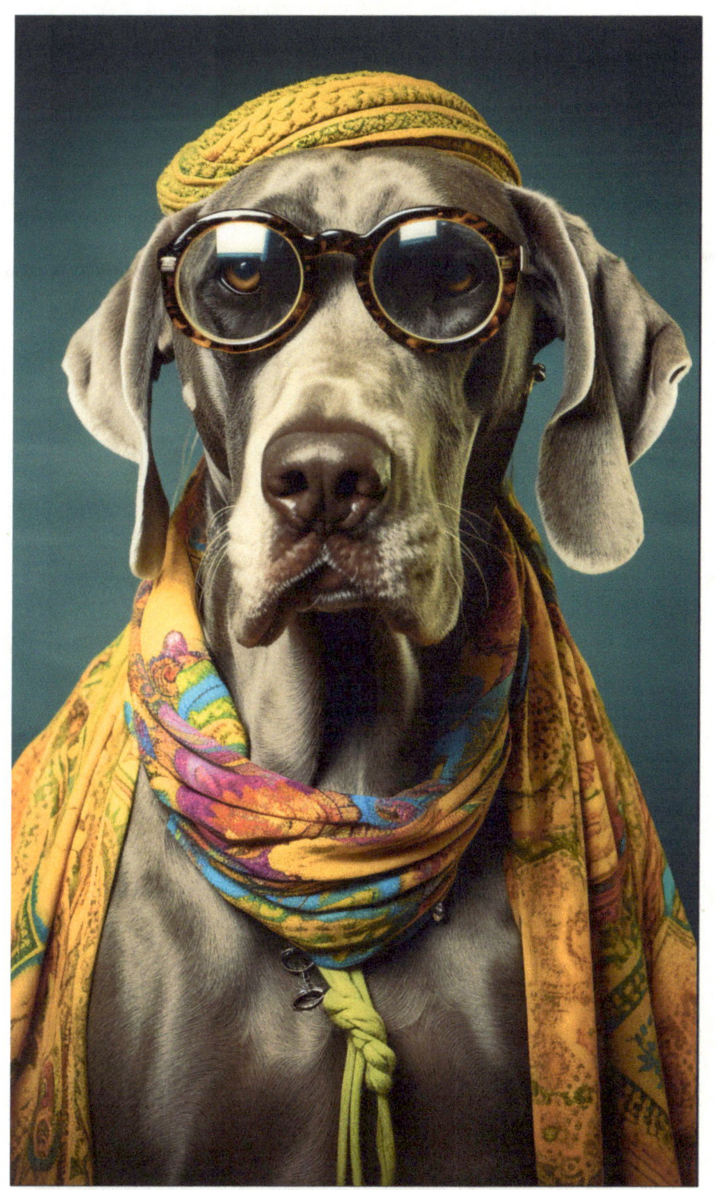
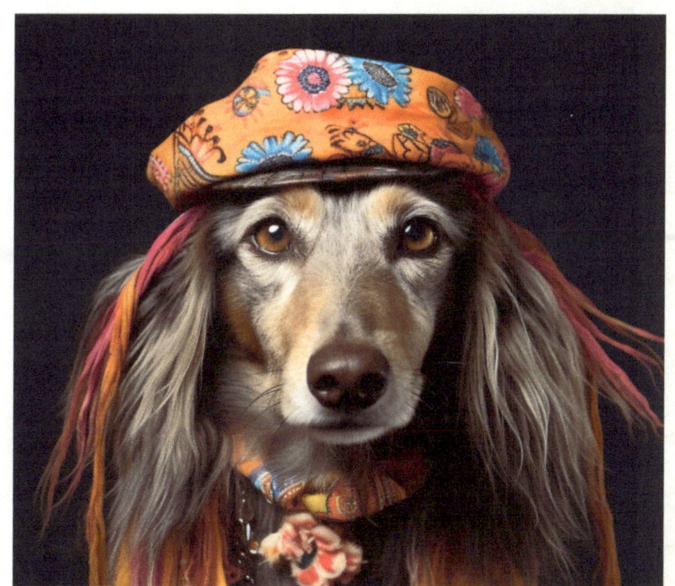
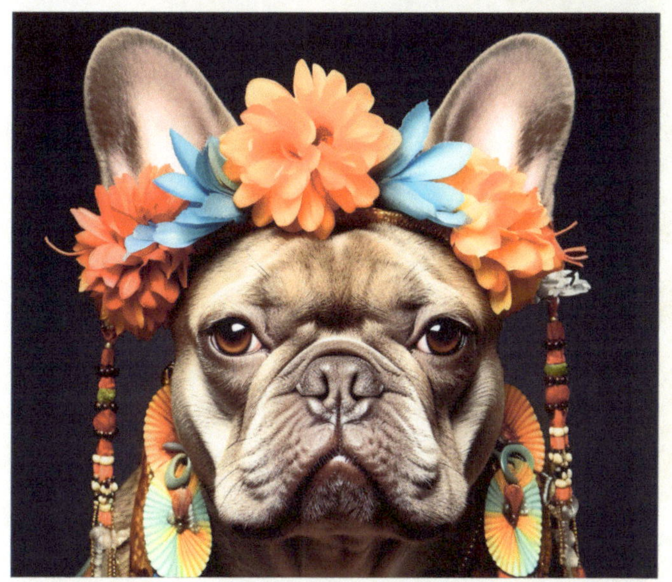
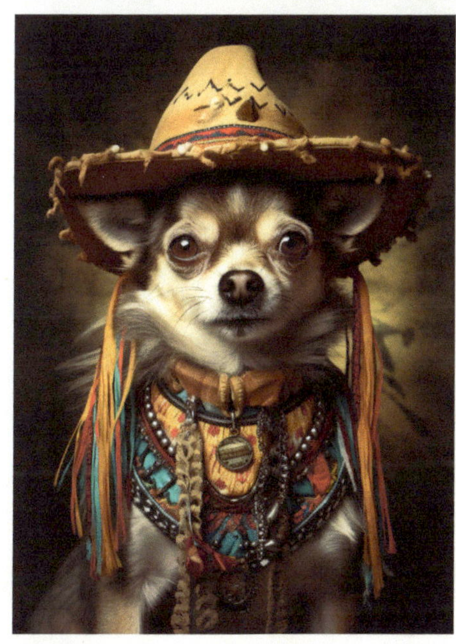
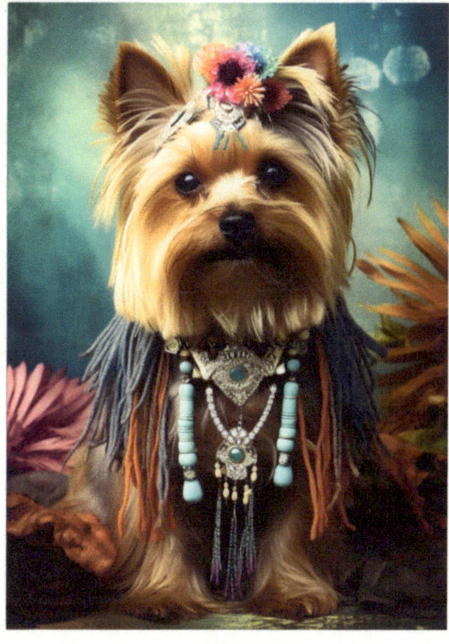
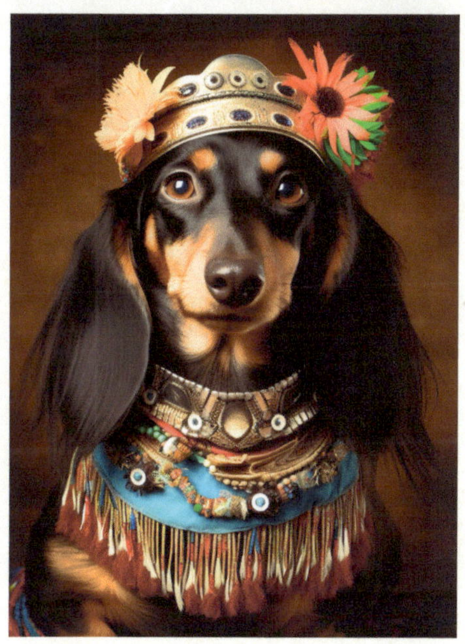

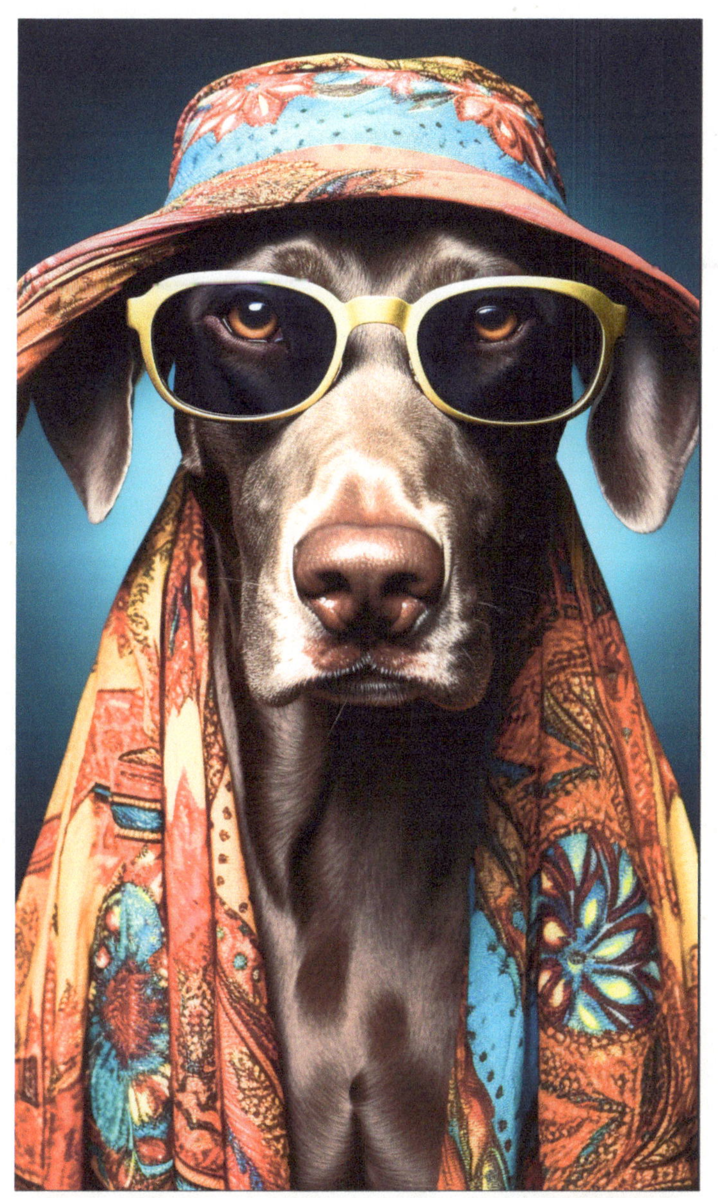
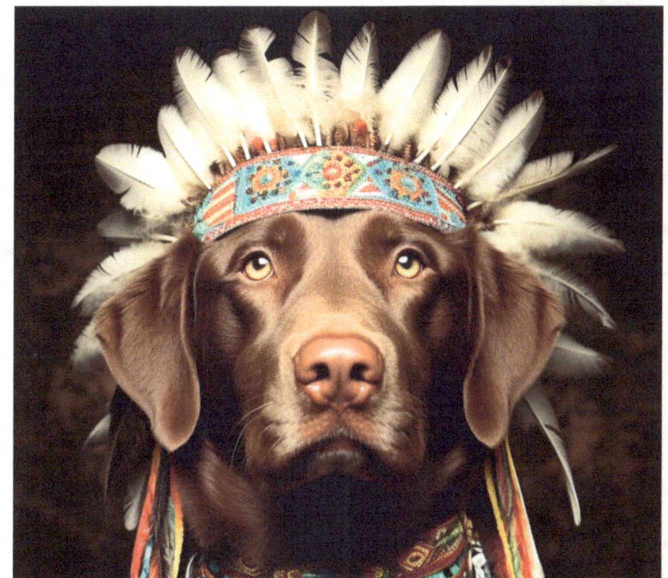
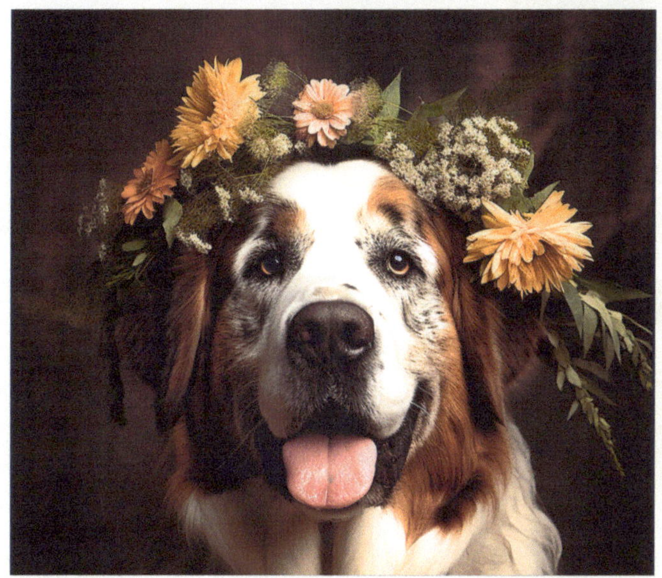
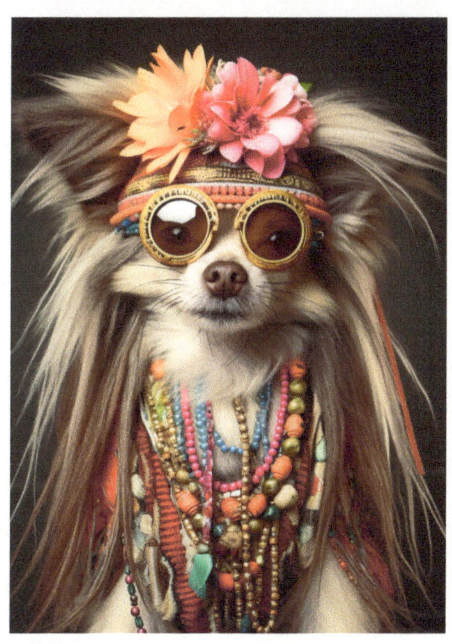
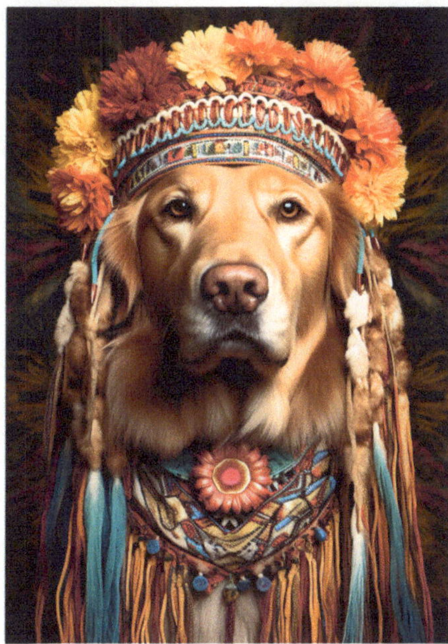
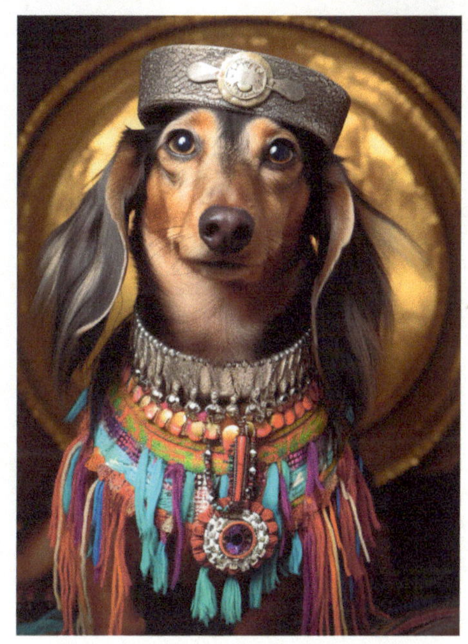

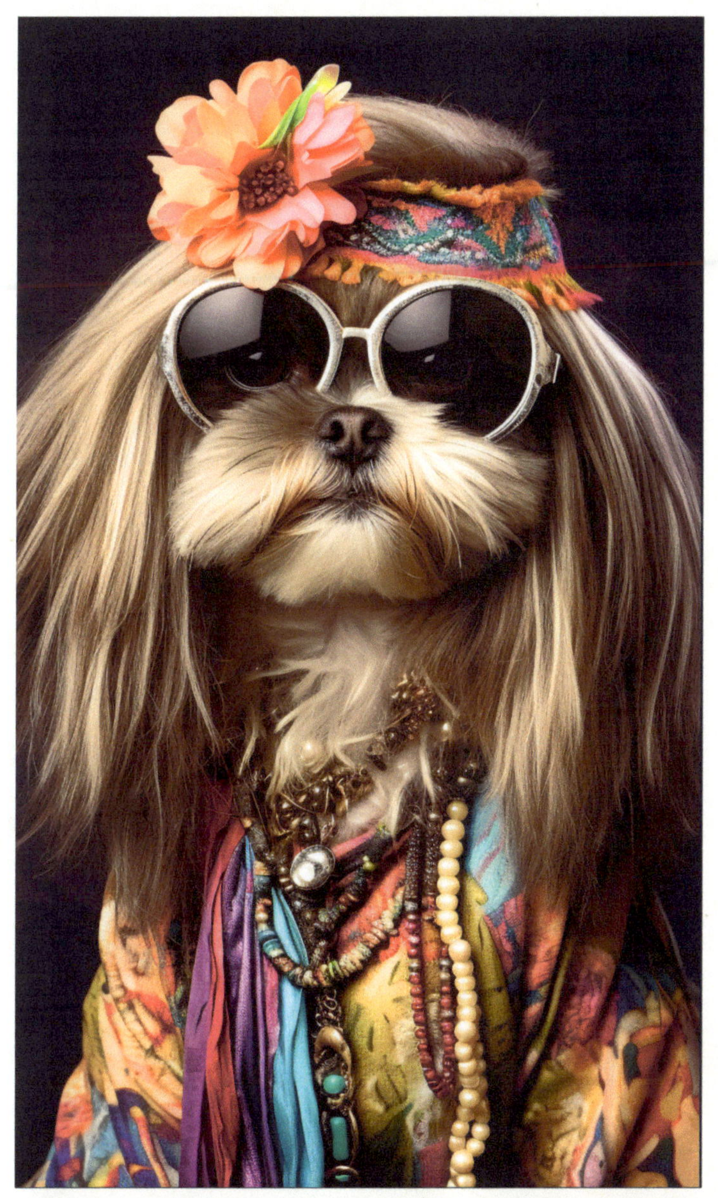
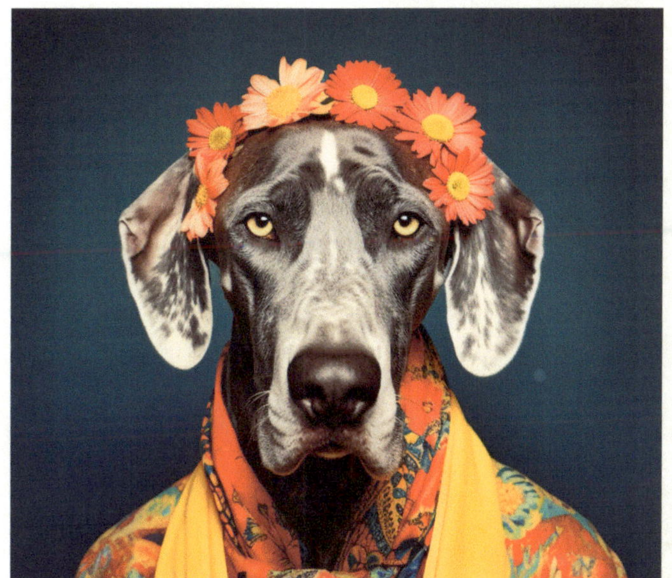
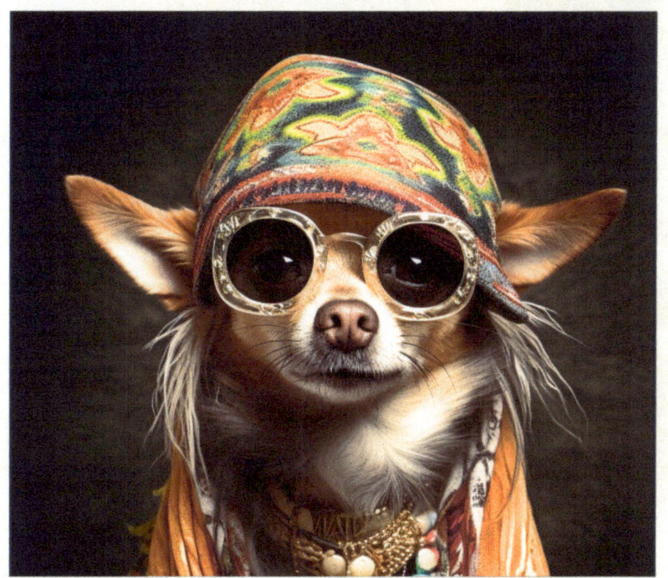
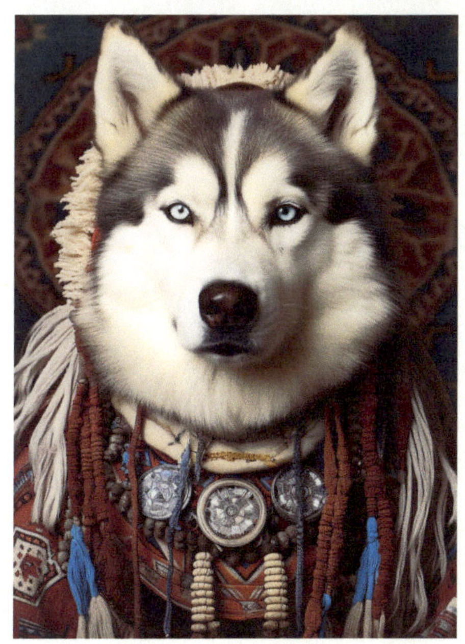
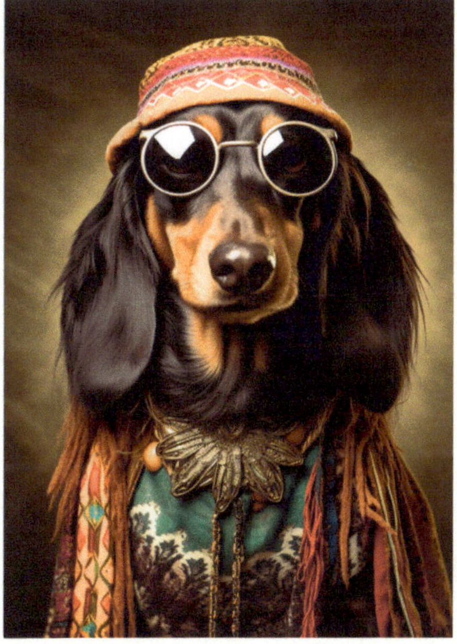
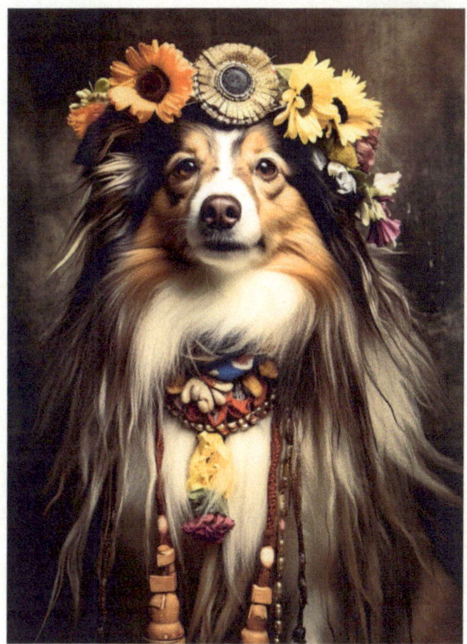

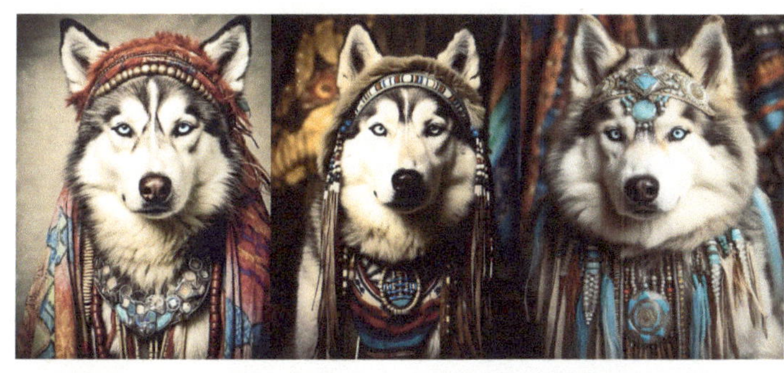
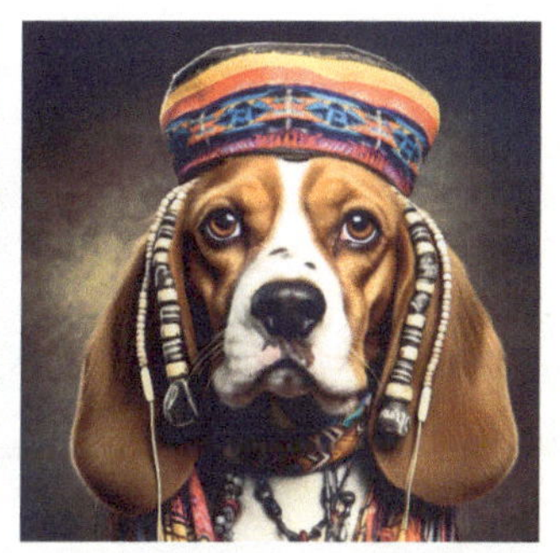
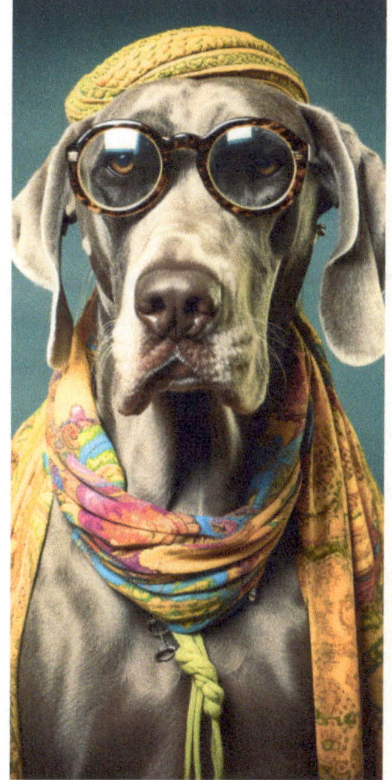
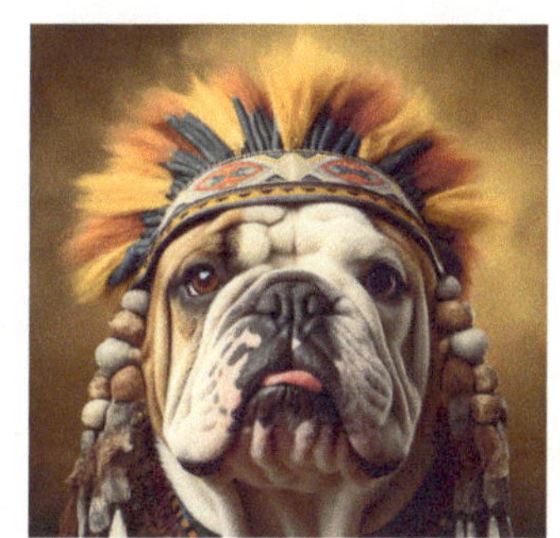
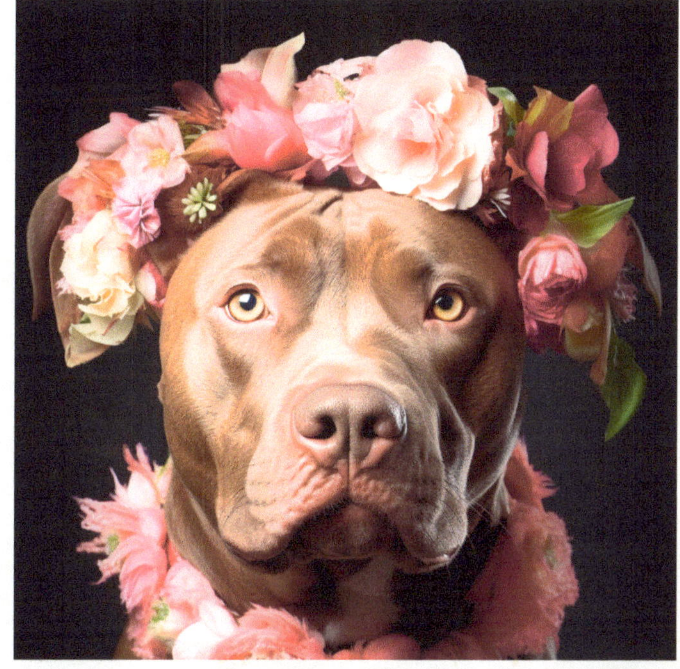
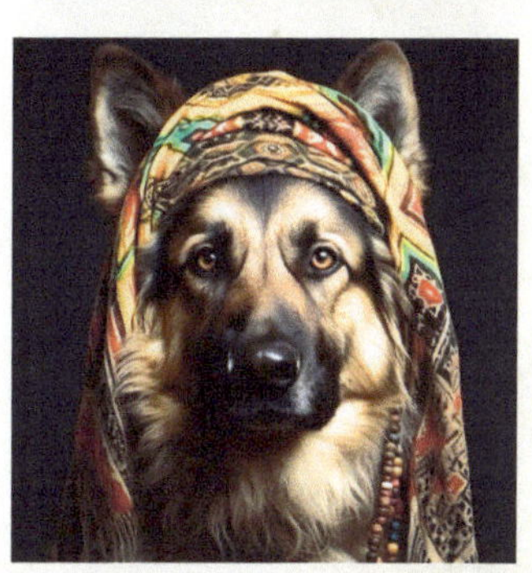
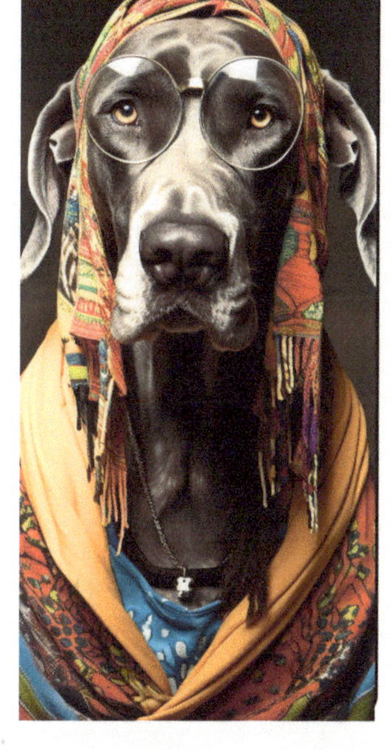
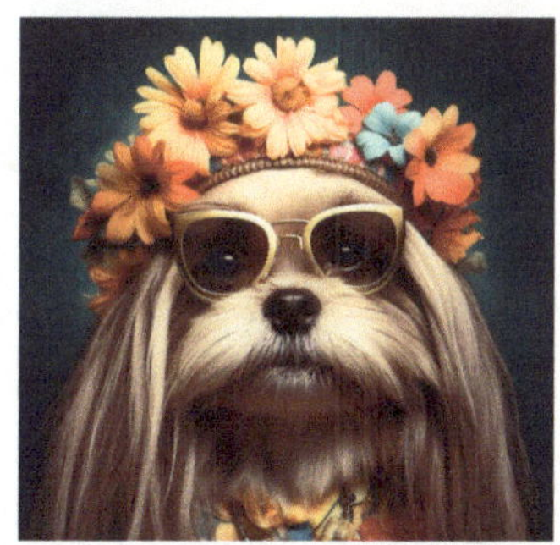
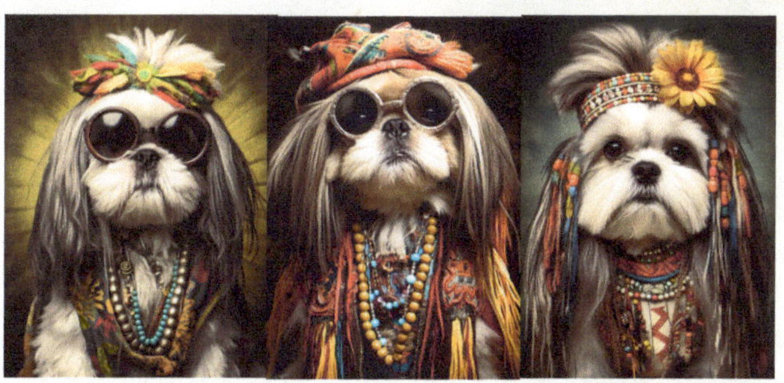
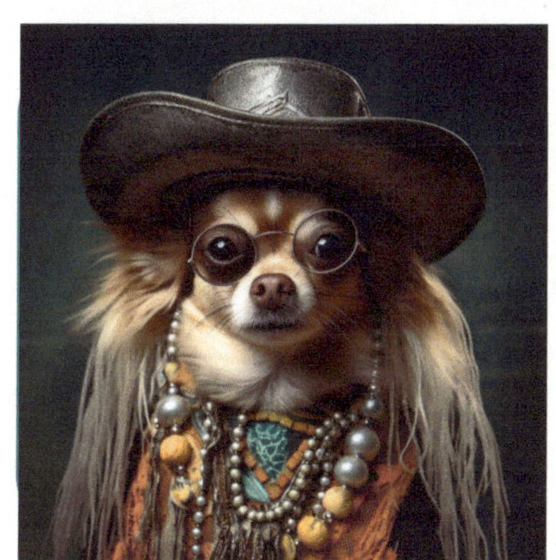
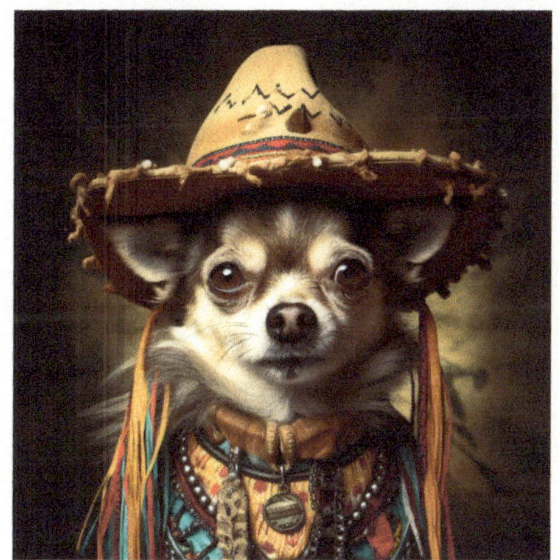
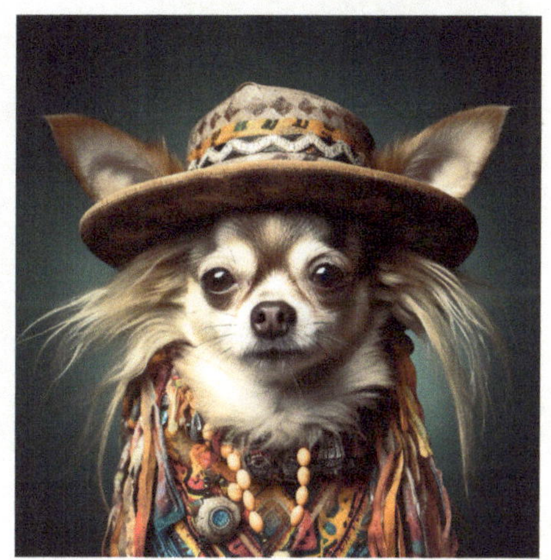

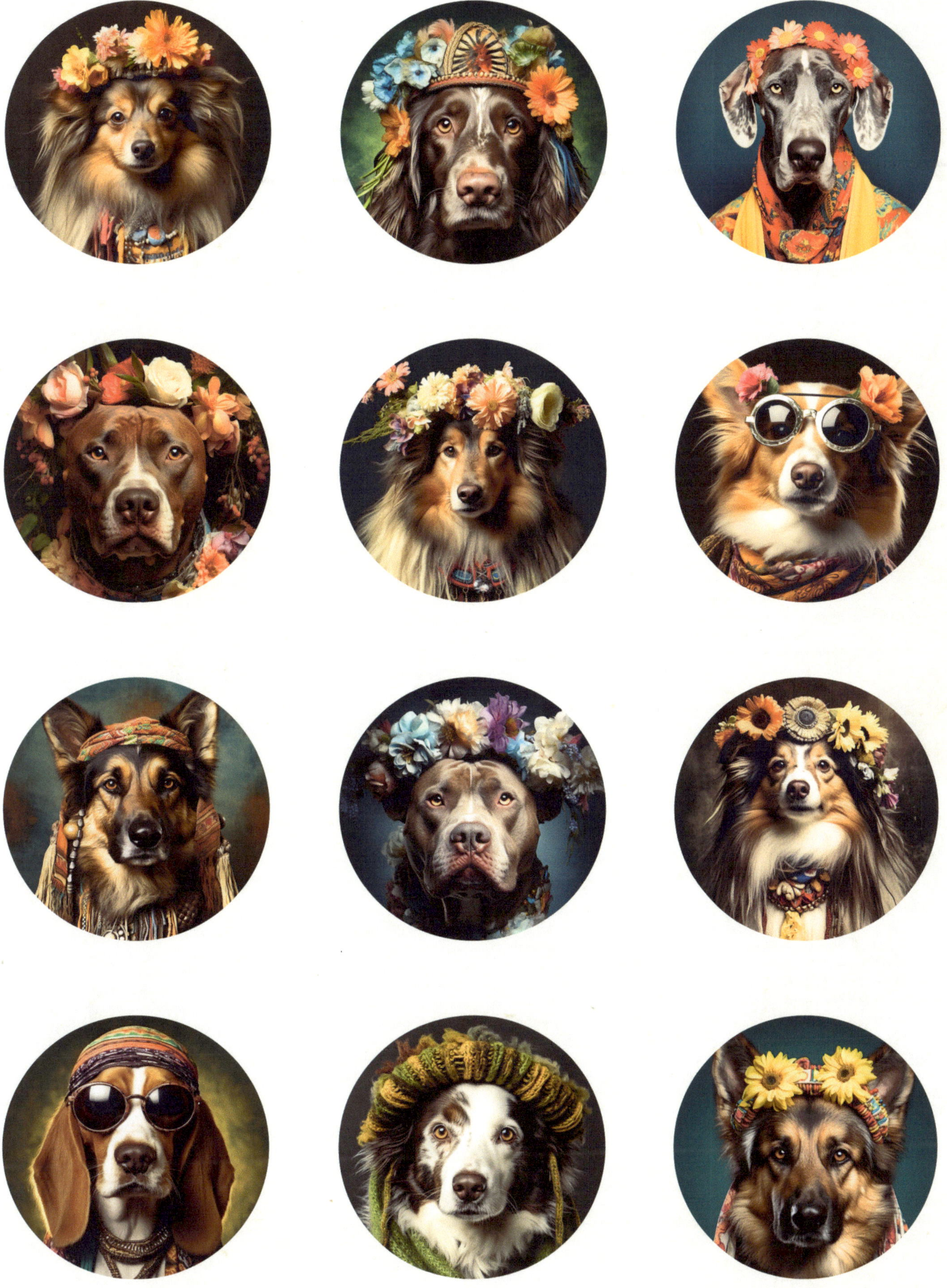

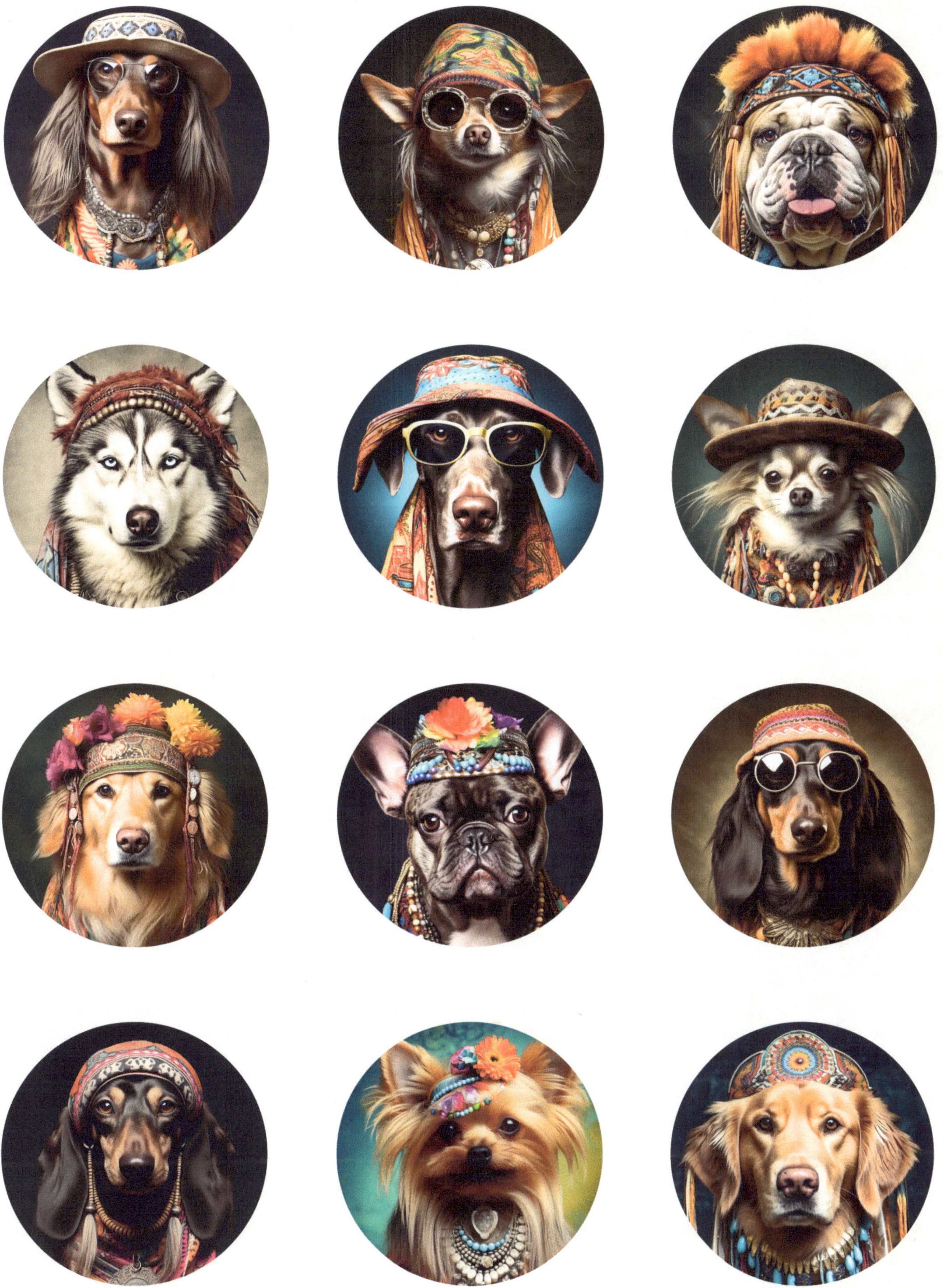

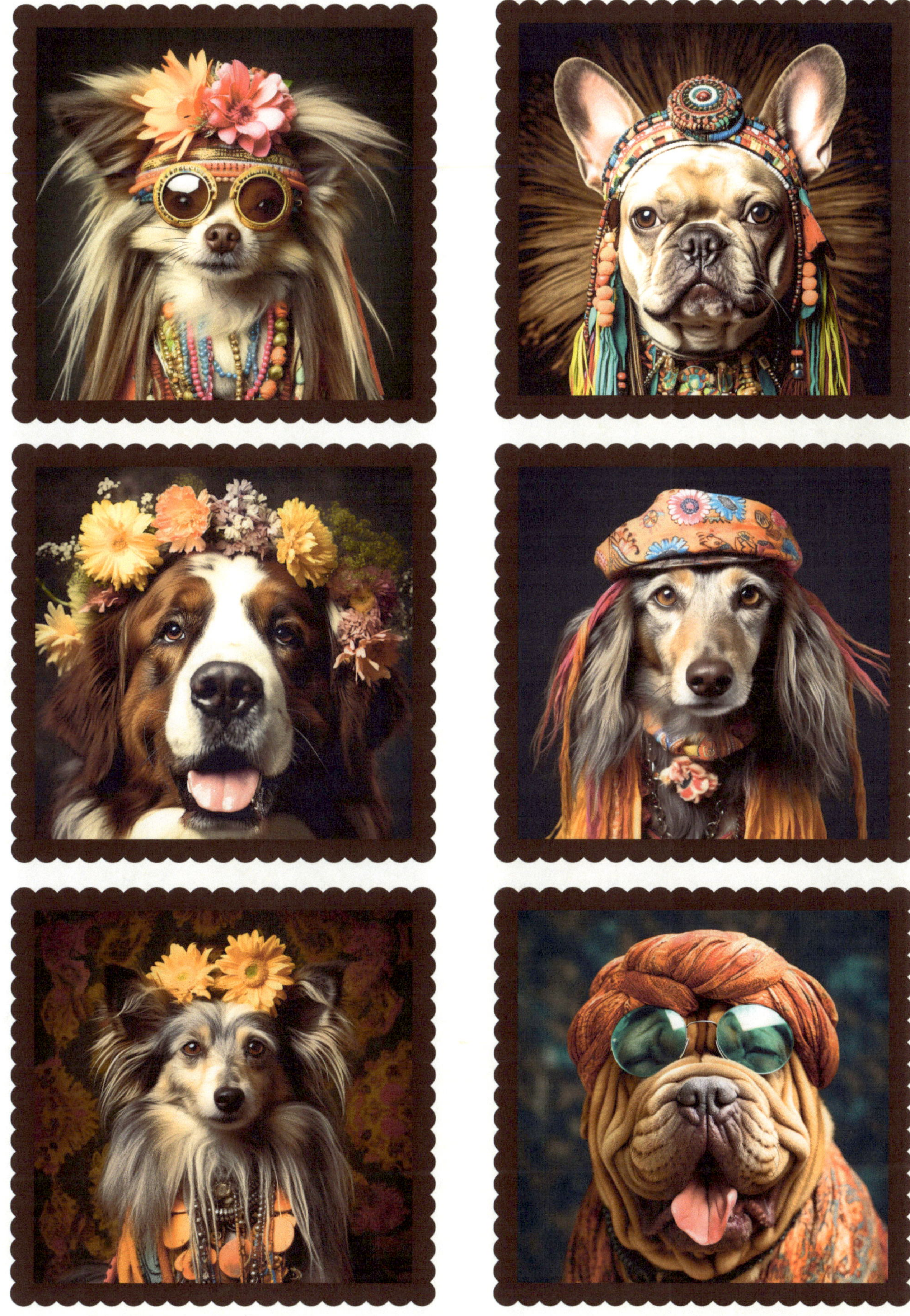

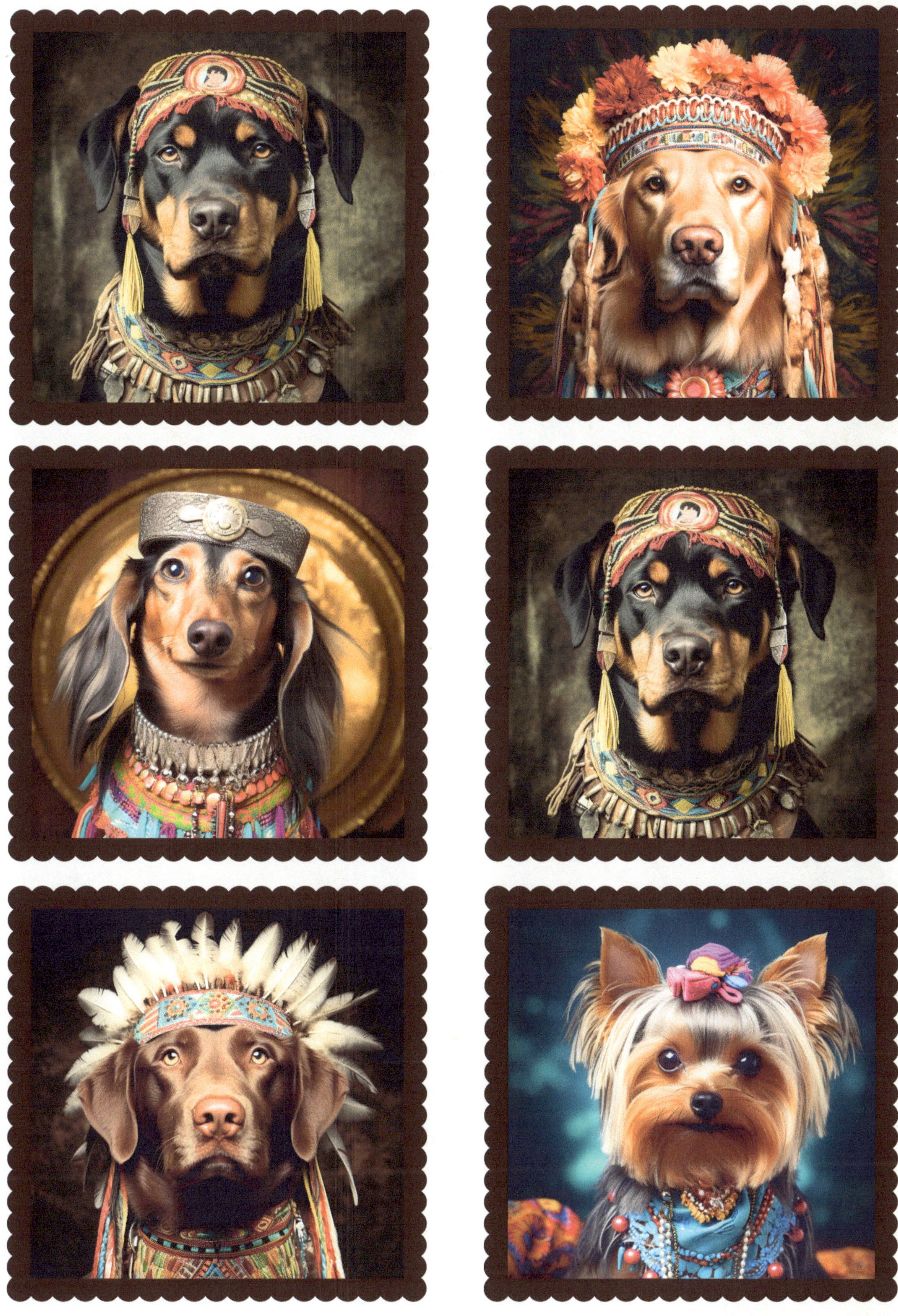

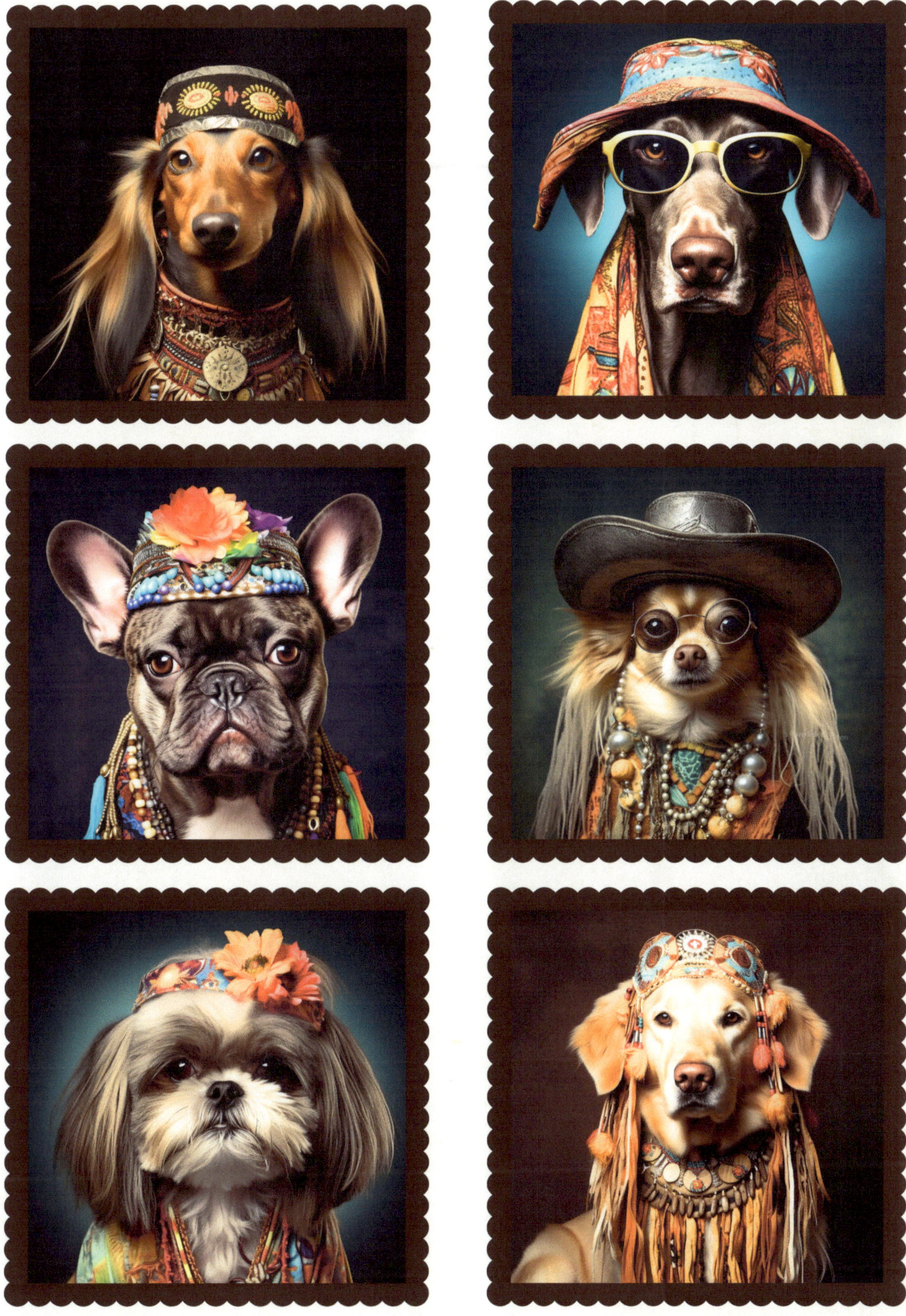

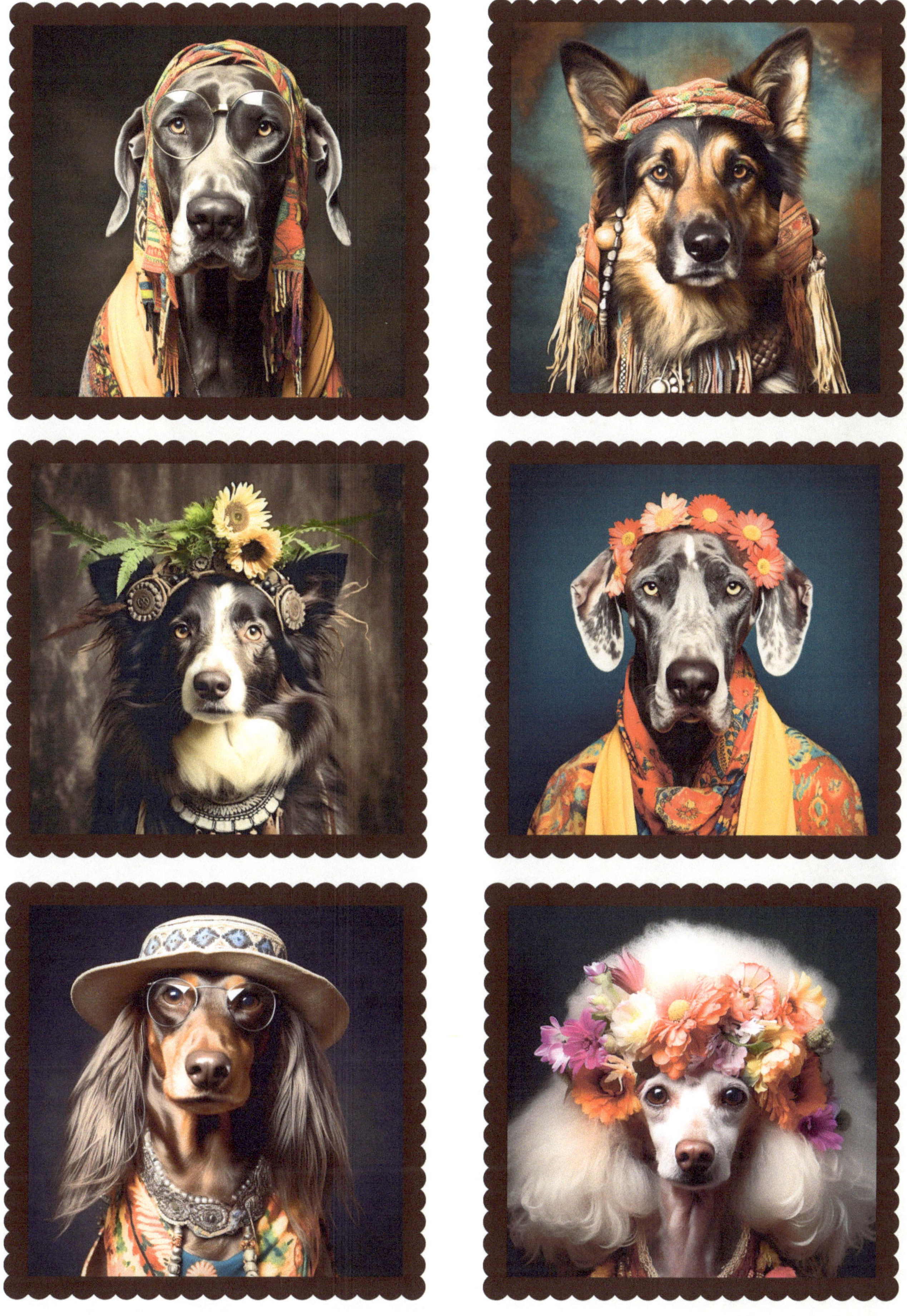

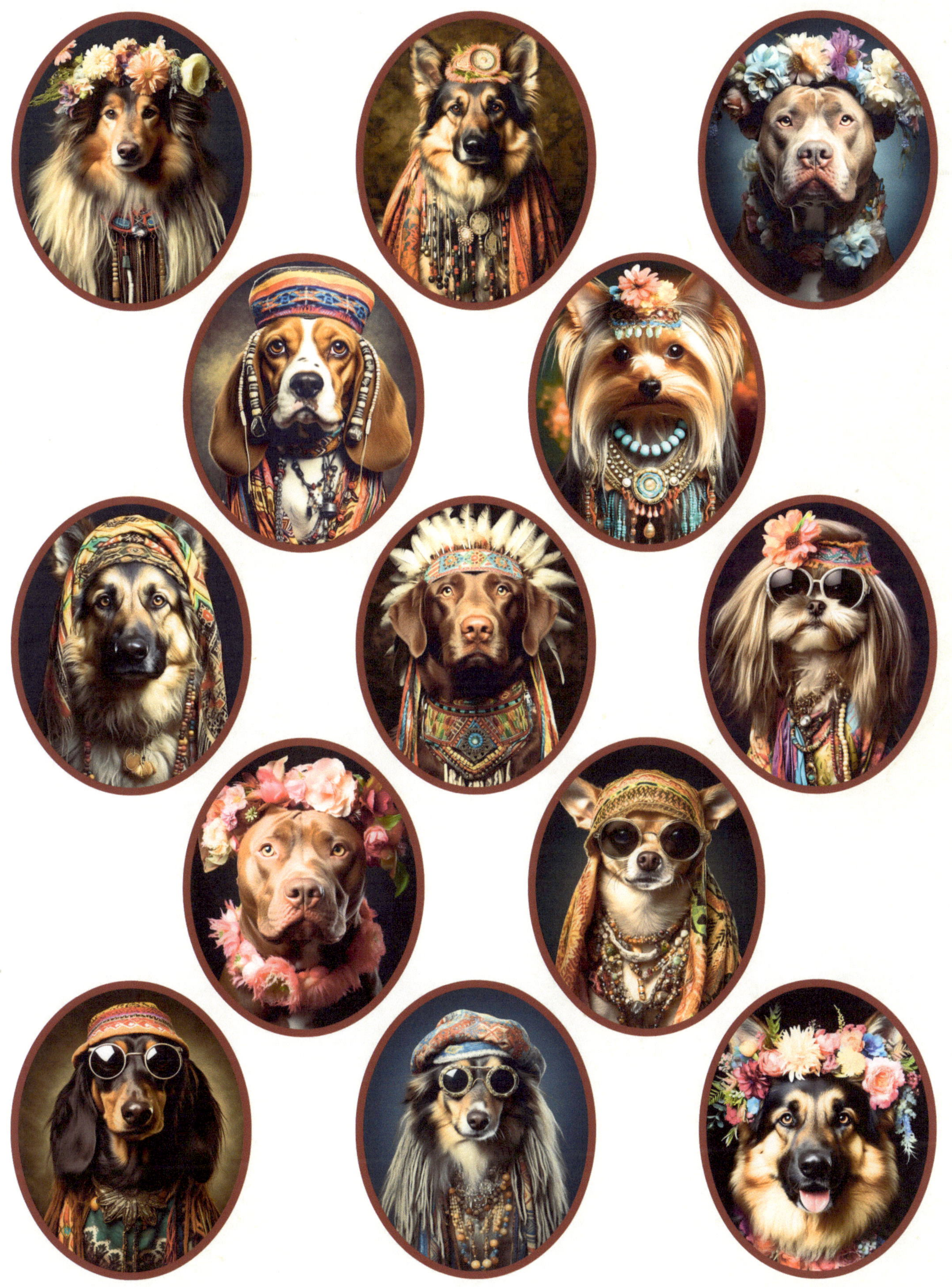

www.ingramcontent.com/pod-product-compliance
Lightning Source LLC
Chambersburg PA
CBHW042116030726
47599CB00002B/242